ADVANCE

"Zeneba Bowers and Matt W̶
the day-to-day routines of ⌐
its culinary traditions. They deliver what every arm-
chair traveler and guidebook devotee is seeking: An in-
delible sense of place and the locals-only advice you
need to experience it for yourself."

> — **ROBERT FIRPO-CAPPIELLO**, Editor in Chief, Budget
> Travel (BudgetTravel.com)

"An indispensable travel companion for first timers, a
must for regulars and, for the amount of golden
nuggets and heaps of cherished information con-
tained, vital for the downright lunatic Italophiles. Let's
give the authors credit for having had the capacity to
dig into the substrata of the region's soul, turn them
upside down and inside out and hash out without pre-
sumption a bounty of surprise hints that can only be
fruit of someone that has a very special bond and love
relation with Italy. Eccellente amici miei!"

> — **DARIO CASTAGNO**, author of *Too Much Tuscan Sun*

"Matt and Zeneba have spent countless hours in the region accumulating invaluable knowledge, at the local
level. They've developed lasting relationships with the
people who run their recommended restaurants and
accommodations. Vital in a great travel plan—they
know the fascinating places of interest, what to see and
do, best routes to take AND the times to avoid! Their
planning guidance made my recent solo trip in Italy,
using only backroads, both flawless and fun!"

> — **RAY LANGTON**, CEO, Envigur International, Ltd.,
> Foreign Executive Retreats

Emilia–Romagna
ITALY

A Personal Guide to Little-known Places
Foodies Will Love

Zeneba Bowers
Matt Walker

Note: Since this is a "Kindle MatchBook" you can download the Amazon Kindle for free, along with any updates, delivered automatically.

Emilia-Romagna, Italy
A Personal Guide to Little-known Places Foodies Will Love

Zeneba Bowers & Matt Walker

F I R S T   E D I T I O N

ISBN: 978-1-942545-19-4
Library of Congress Control Number: 2015951703

All photography by Zeneba Bowers and Matt Walker.
Maps by Laura Atkinson. Book design by Nancy Cleary.

Little Roads Publishing
An Imprint of Wyatt-MacKenzie

www.LittleRoadsEurope.com

Table of Contents

Western Emilia-Romagna
Busseto and the Po River Plains

Western Emilia-Romagna
Castles and Monasteries in the Mountains

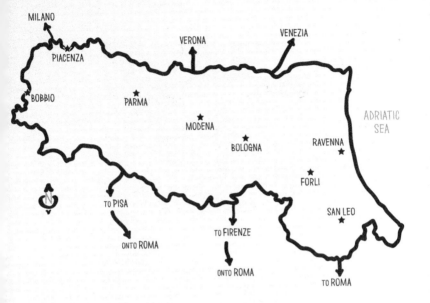

RATINGS KEY

We love all the places we've listed in this book. Our rating system starts pretty high to start; even a 1-star place is a really good place to go.

★	A really good place to go
★★	A really, *really* good place to go
★★★	A **really** great place to go
★★★★	A **really, seriously great** place to go

$$$	higher priced
$$	moderately priced
$	inexpensive; sometimes accepts only cash

OUR GOALS

Wherever we travel, our goals are always the same:

★ Adapting to the culture and interacting with the locals;

★ Experiencing life beyond what one finds as a typical tourist;

★ Slowing down and allowing ourselves time to take in everything around us;

★ Learning about the food, culture and history of the area; and

★ Avoiding tourist crowds whenever possible.

ABOUT THIS BOOK

This is a guidebook for those who wish to get off the beaten track and have an immersive and authentic small-town experience. We delve deeply into the countryside, down the little roads. We find unusual sights, great local restaurants, masterful artisans, and unique lodging, many of which have little or no presence on the Internet or in other guidebooks.

This book is not meant to be a comprehensive, all-inclusive guide to the region. Rather, it is a collection of memorable places that we've found over our years of traveling in Emilia-Romagna. While we provide maps in this book, you'll still want to have a good road map of the region.

The best way to explore the Emilia-Romagna region is by car. This book contains six driving adventures, covering different and diverse regions of Emilia-Romagna. We have created them to be very loose, designed to allow you to go at your own pace, rather than giving specific day-by-day direction. We advise allowing yourself anywhere from a couple of days to a week for each one, and even more time if you have it. In addition, some of them will easily overlap with one another. They can also overlap with the itineraries from our Tuscany guide.

Planning a Trip to Emilia-Romagna

When planning a trip to Italy, the typical tendency is to cover as much ground as possible and see the most important sight — The Leaning Tower, the Colosseum, Venice, the Last Supper. We encourage you to throw out that checklist, as it is the same list as that of thousands of other tourists, An overly-packed schedule is a harsh mistress; if you want a minute-by-minute to-do list, you could have stayed at work. If you want an authentic experience, you need to allow yourself time to have one: Time to have a long lunch, to converse with locals, to explore a side street or an unexpected sight, to relax and breathe.

As itinerary planners, we have talked many clients out of some of the "must-see" destinations in favor of little-known places. They always return rested, fulfilled, and carrying life-long memories of their experiences.

The excursions in this book will guide you through some of the most beautiful countryside, take you to some fascinating locations, and lead you to some of the most delicious food and drink experiences you'll ever find.

Our way of traveling is different

As professional classical musicians, Zeneba is the Artistic Director and Matt is the Operations Manager of the Grammy-nominated ALIAS Chamber

Ensemble. We put a great deal of time and thought into creating interesting and diverse programs for concerts. By the time we founded the group, we had already performed much of the standard and often-heard music by famous composers. We decided to try something more adventurous. As a result the ensemble made a name for itself for commissioning new music, finding and performing great but unusual pieces by little-known composers, and occasionally offering lesser-known works by the great masters. The result became an eclectic concert experience that has something for everyone, while introducing audiences to new ways of listening to music.

When we started traveling to Europe, we applied the same general idea to our travel philosophy: After checking off the obligatory visits to the A-list locations (the Roman Colosseum, the Tower of London, Venice, Stonehenge, and the like), we started looking for more authentic, out-of-the-way experiences. We found them down the little roads of Europe — the small towns, the remote abbeys and castles, the ruins of Roman outposts, and of course the Grandma's-kitchen cuisine. This was a more immersive experience, visiting places without tourists but rich with culture, art, architecture, history, and food.

INTRODUCTION

Emilia-Romagna

Where the Best Things Are Commonplace

The Emilia-Romagna region of northern Italy is often ignored by visitors. Since our first visit, our love for this fascinating region has grown deeper. It is a region rich in history, from ancient Etruscans to Romans to medieval and Renaissance cultures. It contains preserved castles, gorgeous natural scenery, and a wealth of artwork and architecture that spans centuries. And it is the home of some of the culinary cornerstones of Italian cooking.

In 2006 we set off on our honeymoon, which began in Rome, and ended in Venice. We decided to drive from Rome to Venice so we could spend a few days in the idyllic Italian countryside we'd always heard shouldn't be missed. We were looking for something remote, so we decided to spend a few days near the little farming town of Scandiano in Emilia-Romagna, at a countryside *agriturismo*. This was where we discovered what seemed like the real Italian experience: In the ancient small towns, down the far-flung, little roads, away from the tourists, the bright lights and boutique stores, and the traffic. This was the breadbasket of Italy, the source of so much traditional Italian cuisine, starlit nights filled with the songs of crickets, ancient walled castle towns, and the home to so many hard-working people. Reflecting on the trip when we returned home, we realized that, for us, big towns were a bit overwhelming. We craved the peace, authenticity, affordability, and timelessness of the countryside. And the food — always, always, the food.

Our first night in this region, we sat on the patio of a restaurant within walking distance of our *agriturismo*. As we were new to the region, we asked the server for help choosing some wine. We struggled with our limited language skills to ask what's locally made: *"Qualcosa vino rosso locale?"*— literally, "Something red wine location?" But she got the idea; she told us in patient, slow Italian, that the local stuff is a carbonated (*"frizzante"*) wine that's served cold. We didn't understand — we thought she was talking about *prosecco*, the standard Italian sparkling white.

We restated that, while we do indeed enjoy prosecco, in this instance we'd like red, not white, and something that's the usual wine of choice in the area. She sighed, and said again that what we're looking for is indeed red, it is sparkling and served chilled. After a few more rounds of this "Who's On First" routine, we finally comprehended, and were delighted to have discovered *lambrusco*. This is the *vino* of choice in much of Emilia Romagna, made from a grape that has been cultivated in the region since Etruscan times. It's lighter-bodied than, say, a Chianti, and ranges from sweet to very dry. Its effervescence and chill perfectly complements the rich, hearty food of the region.

We told her that we're on our honeymoon — "*luna di miele*" — and she gawked incredulously. We were outside a small farming town in the middle of nowhere — why in the world, she asked, would we come here for our honeymoon? The answer came on the plates she served us — the various *salumi* (cold cuts), the *torta fritta* (fried bread), the balsamic vinegar and *parmigiano reggiano* cheese, the homemade stuffed *tortelli* pastas, the grilled meat dishes. Emilia Romagna is the home of some of the very best of Italian cuisine, and small towns like this are where to find it all at its peak and in its most traditional forms. And it's served with such pride and friendliness — the people here are preparing food from ancient traditions, and they are happy to share with those who appreciate it.

At breakfast ("*colazione*") the next morning in our *agriturismo* lodging, proprietor Anna Brevini had baked several goodies to choose from. After the previous evening's epic meal, we didn't feel a need for much sustenance, but we asked Anna what she typically has. The answer: a couple of chunks of *parmigiano* cheese, a piece of bread and a bit of honey or jam. And to drink? A glass of last night's *prosecco*, a bit flat by morning but still cold and refreshing.

We were happy to eat this fine *parmigiano* for breakfast with some of Anna's homemade jam. Apparently so was one of her farm cats, who came up to beg at our table. Anna yelled at the cat — *"Vai, gattino!"* — who scurried off to the door before looking back wistfully and voicing a pitiful meow. Relenting, Anna tossed a sizeable chunk of the *parmigiano* to the cat, who carried it off and ate it in the yard with what we imagined was great appreciation for the rich granular texture and delicious flavor. It seemed like a perfect illustration that here in the heart of Emilia-Romagna, fine things like this are commonplace.

Later that day we stopped by chance at a modest roadside restaurant; all the patrons here were locals, mostly workers on their lunch hours. (In Italy, "lunch hour" usually lasts for about two.) One of the first things they brought is a large platter of *salumi*, *parmigiano*, and marinated onions; it looked like a deli tray at a wedding reception. "Let's not take too much," Zeneba admonished; "make sure we leave enough for the other diners when they

 pass the tray around." But a moment later we realized our misconception: Every table in the place received an identical tray of these goodies. This "deli tray" is meant for two people, not an entire bridal party. Every bite is made in-house or nearby, sourced locally; the abundance and quality is astonishing. And delicious.

This kind of abundance, we found, is not limited to this region's food. Lovely people, breathtaking scenery, and fascinating historic sites are plentiful. So it was that we unexpectedly discovered Emilia-Romagna, the breadbasket of Italy, far away from the tourist throngs of Rome and Venice. When we looked back on this first trip to Italy, we didn't think of the Roman Forum or the

Grand Canal; rather, we recalled again and again the sweeping landscape of wide-open plains, the starlit nights in the big sky, the ancient towns and medieval castles on every hillside, the delicious food generously served with pride that comes from centuries of tradition. We have been drawn back to this region repeatedly since then, exploring the small towns and back roads, immersing ourselves in the local culture, experiencing an authentic taste of Italy. After many years of travel, we decided to write this book to share our love for Emilia-Romagna, and to share the "Little Roads" style of travel that has become our hallmark.

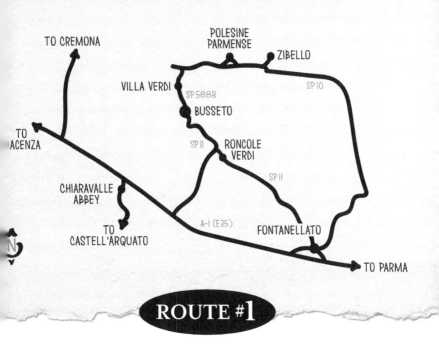

ROUTE #1

Western Emilia-Romagna
Busseto and the Po River Plains

On this route we will experience the upscale cousin of prosciutto ham, and enjoy pork in more forms than we can count; explore the ancestral stomping ground of one of the most famous and influential sons of Italy; examine a fascinating example of medieval surveillance technology in a moated castle; and stroll through a 12th century monastery complex inspired by a bird.

We begin on the flood plains of the Po River, which forms the northern boundary of Emilia-Romagna. The river flows east from its source on Italy's Alpine border with France, down from the foothills and across the plains, and all the way to the Adriatic Sea. Just south of the main A1 Autostrada, we find tiny **Chiaravalle**, a town surrounded by farmlands in all directions. This is the site of the 12th century **Abbazia di Chiaravalle della Colomba**, which boasts a curious origin story: When a group of French Cistercian monks led by St. Bernard were getting ready to establish this monastery, a dove ("*colomba*") flew down to a nearby field, picked up a few twigs, and dropped them on the ground in the shape of a church. The

monks decided to locate their monastery in that field and in that bird-inspired layout.

Whether the architects were in fact avian or human, they designed and built a tremendous and beautiful cathedral and abbey. It was the habit of the Cistercians to move into disadvantaged areas (as this was at the time), establish a presence, and preach the virtues of hard work.

The church itself includes a rose window and impressive vaulted ceilings, with distinctive pink and white striped brick-work in the arches and doorways. The interior nave and aisles are stark and only sparsely adorned — St. Bernard disapproved of ornate medieval decoration and especially the fantastic bestiary that we see in contemporaneous churches. However, the altar and organ areas and the chapels contain some beautiful old statuary, frescoes, wood carvings, and paintings. In May and June, the church hosts an *infiorata* — an ornate and complex display in which artists decorate the floors and walkways with millions of flower petals, depicting and framing biblical scenes.

The cloister next door — a square, open garden space surrounded by covered walkways — has some intricately carved stonework. Its architecture is numerologically laid out — seven arches on each side for the days of the week, 52 columns for the number of weeks in the year, and so forth. Look for the monk figures carved in stone in two of the corners, apparently shouldering the weight of the structure. The inside square is supported by distinctive "knotted" columns, each carved from a single block of pink marble so it appears to be four smaller columns that are knotted together like ropes. (The church in San Quirico d'Orcia in Tuscany has these same knotted columns; this design can be seen scattered throughout the continent, especially in Cistercian buildings.)

Traveling north from Chiaravalle, we come to **Busseto** and walk up the Via Roma into the *centro*. This main street is lined on both sides with portico

walkways, leading us in shaded comfort past shops, apartments, grocers and bars to the main square. Here we stop in at **Caffe Centrale**, right on the corner of the *piazza*, for an espresso or grappa and a bite to eat. The cafe is wholly dedicated to opera, with a huge collection of signed, framed head-shots of opera stars past and present. The interior of the bar is more highly decorated than most: velvet covered chairs, mahogany inlaid ceilings, chandeliers, marble tabletops. The bar's counter has a wide selection of upscale artisanal chocolates to choose from, as well as fresh pastries and cookies.

Sufficiently caffeinated, we step back out onto the main square, where the bar's opera fixation becomes readily apparent: The **Piazza Giuseppe Verdi**, named for the town's favorite son. The square is dominated by a statue of the famous 19th-century composer in front of the imposing **Teatro Verdi**, a former fortress that dates back as far as the 10th century. The actual theater is housed in the castle structure, and is itself surprisingly small (about 300 seats) but lavishly decorated. All

the wood is carved to look like hanging beads or painted to look like marble. It is easy to see why the socialites of Verdi's time regarded Busseto's exclusive opera world with such high esteem — everyone who came to the performances here must have felt like they were steeped in the height of luxury.

Verdi was born not in Busseto but just a few kilometers away, in the tiny village of **Le Roncole** (now referred to as Roncole Verdi, because, fame). He is famously (perhaps spuriously) quoted as saying, "I am and always will be a peasant ('*paesano*') from Roncole." Verdi's childhood home is open for tours as a museum, where visitors can see the humble roots from which this musical icon sprang. His father was the keeper of a crossroads inn and general store here, much of which is still intact. Down the street is the town's 11th-century Church of St Michael the Archangel, where Verdi

Verdi and Italian Unification

The country we now know as Italy only became Italy as a result of the *Risorgimento* — the tumultuous period of Italian unification in the 19th century. Previously, the peninsula was an assortment of monarchies and city-states controlling various regions. Verdi and his music played an important part in the unification: Several of his operas had not-too-subtle political overtones, favoring democracy over the abuse of power that came with monarchy and oligarchy. Since the country was unified during the height of Verdi's fame, his music became the quintessential national music of the Italian people.

was baptized — the same baptismal font is still there and used to this day.

The estate of the composer at the height of his fame is located a few kilometers in the opposite direction, a bit northwest of Busseto in Sant'Agata. **Villa Verdi** is grand, with many Verdi artifacts (his piano, opera scores, the famous bust, and other memorabilia) on display. The grounds are extensive and beautiful, and include flowered gardens, a lake with a small island, a cave carved from the local *tufa* rock, and a large number of tree species that will impress dendrologists.

Clearly there is an abundance of good sightseeing in this area; fortunately, there are also a couple of excellent, off-the-beaten-track restaurants just minutes away. Driving directly north, we cross these open farmlands until we reach the Po River and the small, unassuming town of **Polesine Parmense**, home to the excellent restaurant **Il Cavallino Bianco**. The place began as a modest food stall at a busy river crossing in the 1920s, serving travelers waiting for passage; the location became so popular that they later added a dance floor and a kitchen. Bands would play and the locals would come to dance, as well as to eat and drink. During the war, the Nazis occupied the town and the place was closed down, and in 1951 it was destroyed by a flood of the Po River. Rebuilt a year later, it became

the quintessential example of farm-to-table cooking. All of the food is homemade, sourced from their own farms, vineyards, and orchards. Among the specialties is various types of pork, gloriously featured in their annual "November Porc" celebration: This is a fixed price menu, featuring pork as many ways as one can imagine, all of them delicious, along with house wines.

The offerings are equally tasty in the remaining eleven months: Beautiful handmade pastas with delicate sauces; cold cuts made in-house and cut to order; a perfectly cooked risotto made with a reduction of the house *lambrusco*; and their signature chicken dish, "Suprema di Cappone di Giuseppe Verdi". An order of this dish comes with a limited-edition hand-painted ceramic plate to take home as a souvenir. The dining room is elegant, with pressed white linen tablecloths, gleaming wine glasses, and impeccable service. After finishing the embarrassment of riches that is your meal, take a few minutes to browse the attached farm shop to see what you might bring home: Bottles of Cavallino Bianco's wine (made from their own vineyards), their house-made *bargnolino* or *nocino*, or possibly some of their deli-

cious cheeses or *salumi*. A visit to this store will make you wish you brought more bubble wrap.

The various cured meats of this general region are famous, especially the *prosciutto* of Parma. More locally known, though, and regarded as superior, is *culatello*. It is made from the best part of the pig's leg, it takes longer to cure, it can only be made by those with the proper expertise, and has to be made to exacting standards to receive the DOP label of **Zibello**. This tiny village is just a short 5 kilometers to the west, where we find the vine-covered patio of **Trattoria La Buca**.

The women will make you feel welcome here, as if you're eating in your grandma's house; they are proud of the plates they produce, including an old but seldom-seen recipe from the region: A

Culatello di Zibello and the DOP label

Many foods in Italy are labeled with acronyms. These are marks of quality foods produced to exacting standards, like DOC or DOCG (*Denominazione di Origine Controllata e Garantita*) for wine; or IGP (*Indicazione Geografica Protetta*) for various foodstuffs specific to certain geographic regions, like chestnuts of the Apennines. The standards are maintained by various consortiums nationwide. Real *culatello di Zibello* is designated DOP, standing for *Denominazione d'Origine Protetta*. The classification speaks to the production process, which is complex and very specific; it includes salting, tying up with twine in a particular fashion, and even massaging the meat.

savory macaroni dish baked with a sweet, crunchy pie crust, resembling a Greek style *pasticcio*. But the star here is the plate of *culatello*: Translucently thin slices served with crusty bread, fresh butter, and, in the summer, a  couple of juicy, peeled fresh figs. This is an ideal place for us; frequented by locals, focused on artisanal cuisine, a casual and relaxed family atmosphere, and in a tiny town down a tiny road.

After lunch we are invited to see the cantina, the dark cellar where they cure their meats and age barrels of their various wines. This room has an almost overwhelming scent, emanating from 500 years of stone and wood and carefully cultivated yeasts and molds. Dozens of *culatello* hams hang from the low ceiling beams, waiting for at least 12 months before they are ready to be sliced and eaten. We promise to come back and eat them all if we can. La Buca also offers a few rooms for overnight lodging, allowing for eating and drinking to your heart's content.

Historically, this part of the Po valley was part of the Duchy of Parma and Piacenza, so the towns in between these cities feature many old castles. A particularly grand example is in the central town square of **Fontanellato**, home to the **Rocca Sanvi-**

tale. This 14th century fortress (portions of it date to the 12th century) is one of only a handful of Italian castles still surrounded by a moat, and accessible over a single drawbridge. Visitors can explore a labyrinthine series of rooms, including a billiard room, a library, and an armor room.

Many of these spaces have ornate 16th-century frescoes depicting weird pastoral scenes — cherubs with wry, knowing expressions, pipe-playing satyrs, maidens bathing, dogs chasing a deer, a hunter with a stag's head.

Unique to this fortress, though, is the ***camera ottica*** — literally "optical chamber", though we think of it as "hidden camera". It's a room set in one of the squat outer guard towers, in which a series of mirrors and a prism projects a live image of the comings and goings of the people on the central *piazza* outside the castle — an ingenious predecessor of today's surveillance cameras.

Keeping this in mind, we walk outside to the porticoed walkways around the town square. There are many dining options in this small but bustling town, including the locally

famous **Locanda Nazionale**, just on the other side of the moat. Though specializing in traditional Emiliana regional cuisine, the owner occasionally tries to sneak in a few "modernisms". When we visited, he sat down with us and talked at length of his ideas about food: He had visited the States several times, and was taken with the variety of food that is available. In contrast, he said, his native cuisine is "really excellent, but always the same". His efforts to add new elements to his Italian menu were met by his neighbors with reactions ranging from skepticism to hostility; people there just want their tried and true dishes, without invasions from other cultures. Even his take on that decidedly un-Italian dish familiar to most American diners, the chicken Caesar salad, was too much of a stretch for the locals, despite fresh, locally-grown greens, excellent balsamic vinegar, shaved *parmigiano* cheese, and chicken grilled over a wood flame. For those of us who were not born and brought up with this cuisine, though, such departures from the norm are welcome, especially if they still include all of the best local ingredients — and the Po River plains are rich with these.

Polesine Parmense

Il Cavallino Bianco ★★★★ $$$
DESTINATION RESTAURANT

Fantastic restaurant, very popular with locals, in the hamlet of Polesine Parmense. Excellent traditional cuisine, nearly all sourced from their own farms, year-round. In November they offer a special menu (reservation required), called "November Porc", which is a multi-course menu devoted to pork. Great for us, not so great for the local pigs.

Reservations are encouraged.

Closed Tuesdays and January 7-24.

http://www.ristorantealcavallinobianco.it

Zibello

Trattoria La Buca ★★★★ $$

A not-to-be-missed restaurant in tiny Zibello, the home of the 'king' of salumi, culatello. See their cantina filled with curing culatelli and other salumi, plus their own wines. Ask nicely and they may let you see it; worth it for the smells alone. In the summer there is a large patio shaded by wisteria; in cooler months a cozy dining room.

Closed Tuesday. Reservations encouraged. No credit cards.

http://www.trattorialabuca.com

Fontanellato

Locanda Nazionale ★★★ $$$

Located just across the moat from the castle at Fontanellato. Excellent food, occasionally with a modern twist. Outdoor seating in the piazza during warmer months.

Closed Monday.

Polesine Parmense

Il Cavallino Bianco - Bottega ★★★★ $$

If you don't eat at this stellar restaurant, at least stop in at their store next door to stock up on meats, cheeses, oil, wine, liquori, baked goodies, and more. All locally-sourced and homemade, the goods here are the best the region has to offer.

Closed Tuesdays and January 7-24.

http://www.ristorantealcavallinobianco.it

Chiaravalle

Abbazia di Chiaravalle della Colomba ★★★
    Beautiful Cistercian Abbey in the countryside, with lovely cloisters and garden. Also a shop where the monks' products are sold.
    Open 8:30-12 and 2:30-6:30. Free entry.

Busseto

Teatro Verdi ★★ $
    An all-wood theater housed in the Rocca in Busseto; dominates the town square. Rebuilt in the 1860's, today open for guided tours, which are offered in English and Italian. Tickets are €4.
    Closed Monday. Open Tuesday-Friday 10:00-7:00 and Saturday 10:00-2:00.

Sant'Agata

Villa Verdi ★★ $$
    Verdi's mansion just north of Busseto, where he lived for 50 years. Beautiful grounds, and plenty of Verdiana, including his death mask.
    Closed Mondays. €9 entry.
    Opening times vary by season, full information in English can be found here:
http://www.villaverdi.org/pagine/en.php

Roncole

Verdi's Birth House ★★ $

Birthplace of Giuseppe Verdi. This small house was for many years a cantina run by Verdi's family. Tours are offered in Italian and occasionally in English, but English pamphlets are always available.

€5 entry.

In general, closed Mondays, and open other days in the morning and mid- to late-afternoon. Times vary by season, full list can be found here: http://www.casanataleverdi.it

Fontanellato

Rocca Sanvitale ★★★ $

One of the few castles left with a working moat and drawbridge. Also be sure to check out the *camera obscura* inside, with its series of mirrors projecting a real-time image of the street and its people.

€7 entry. Opening times vary by season; generally open mornings and late afternoons. Full times listed here: http://www.coopculture.it/heritage.cfm?id=106#

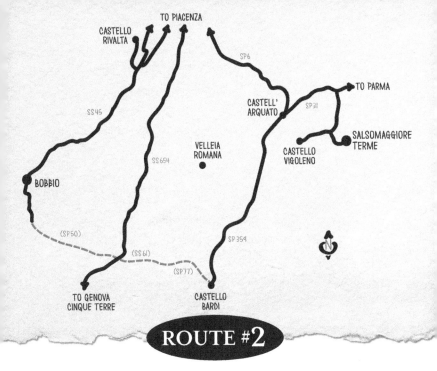

ROUTE #2

Western Emilia-Romagna

Castles and Monasteries in the Mountains

On this route we will explore ancient hilltop fortresses and the ruins of a Roman outpost; see the landscape that is said to have inspired the Mona Lisa; discover liquor made from chamomile; visit a monastery founded by a missionary and saint of Ireland; and dine in a farm-to-table restaurant in a castle popular with the British royal family.

The northern Apennine mountain chain is a rugged region covered in forest and rich in history. The many peaks offered positions of strategic importance over the centuries, which led to the building of impressive and extravagant castles.

Driving south from Piacenza on the SP7 and then the SP40 until it reaches the Trebbia River, we stumble upon one such castle: the stunning **Castello di Rivalta**. Highlighted by its distinctive, fairytale-like round tower, the fortress itself sits within a tiny medieval walled village, which now includes a couple of bars, a large church, a couple of shops, and one of the best restaurants in this entire region. Before lunch at this excellent restaurant, you'll want to proceed to the castle for a tour.

It's possible to arrange in advance for a guided tour with an English-speaking guide; this is well worth the effort and the cost. This site is complex, with many rooms including the great hall, the main dining room, several bedrooms, the wine cellar, the dungeons, and the kitchens. The apex of the tour is of course climbing the round tower, from the top of which we are rewarded with a 360-degree view of the Trebbia valley and, on a clear day, the distant Alps to the north. There are also two interesting museum installations within the castle: A chronological display of Italian uniforms and equipment through the centuries; and an extensive collection of weaponry, armor, and artifacts from the Battle of Lepanto (1571), including the banner that flew on the flagship on the day of the battle. Many of the local families took part in this naval conflict in Greece, in which a coalition of Catholic nations beat back the forces of the Ottoman Empire and prevented them from spreading any farther across southern Europe.

After the hour-long tour, we enjoy a bit of wandering around the quiet, peaceful village. We end up at the door of **Antica Locanda del Falco**. To the left is their *bottega*, an excellent farm store filled with local goodies of all kinds. We'll visit the store later; for now, we take a seat in the restaurant for one of the best lunches anywhere.

Warm days offer the possibility of dining outside here, amid the medieval structures and 100-year-old vines. The interior is all wood beams and terracotta floors. It is a favorite haunt of the locals, but also friendly to *stranieri* (foreigners) like us. Food ranges from traditional plates — tiny *raviolini* stuffed with rabbit, pork and beef;

or a savory veal *Milanese* — to more modern dishes, like an antipasto of lake sturgeon, served with a delicious sauce of parsley, lime, capers and garlic. A visit to del Falco is like tasting the season on a plate — everything comes fresh from local farms and shops, and changes according to the time of year. In spring, we loved the salad made from shaved raw *carciofi* (artichoke) in a vinaigrette. In autumn or winter, look for the *crema castagne* dessert, a dish of local chestnuts and ricotta whipped into a sweet cloud.

Passing through the hallway on the way next door to the *bottega*, we see old photos and articles on the wall documenting the decades of history of the establishment and its proprietors. The store itself is a treasure trove of foodstuffs representing all the best things of the region — fresh produce, cheeses, wines, meats, jams, honeys, chocolates, *liquori*. One visit to this store is enough to understand why we recommend packing an empty duffel bag when traveling to Italy.

We continue south, plunging still deeper into the mountains. After some 30 kilometers winding along the Trebbia River valley, we come to the ancient town of **Bobbio**. Founded as an abbey in 614 AD by Columbanus, a revered saint of Ireland, it is now a small but bustling market town as well as a pilgrimage destination.

We climb the hill to reach the abbey and its 15th century **Basilica di San Colombano**. The arch over the doorway to the church has these words for those who would enter: "*Terribilis est locus iste*". The translation isn't quite as ominous as one would think: "This place is  awesome" is really the idea. These monks were not fooling around with impressions, though: The interior of the church is filled with painted and sculpted images not just of the usual figures of Christian lore, but also of fantastical beasts and

 demon-creatures that were meant to strike fear into the hearts of those who beheld them. Below the altar is a crypt containing the tomb of Columbanus; on the way down, be sure to admire the large 12th-century mosaic flooring, depicting knights in battle against fearsome dragons.

At Bobbio's **Piazza Duomo** stands the town's Romanesque cathedral, dedicated to **Santa Maria Assunta**. Built in 1075 and altered variously over several centuries, it is full of ornate and impressive interior architecture, and many paintings and sculptures depict the heroism and piety of the venerated saints and martyrs. Among them is Saint Vitus — pictured there with his pet lion — whose name lives on in modern medicine for a neurological disorder, St. Vitus' Dance. In addition to being able to ward off animal attacks (hence the lion thing), Vitus is the patron saint of dancers and epileptics.

The main attraction here, as if these ancient holy places were not enough, is the **Ponte Gobbo**,

the "Hunchbacked Bridge". It is a long footbridge crossing the Trebbia River at the edge of town. Built in the 15th century when the original Roman-era bridge was washed out in a flood, it consists of eleven uneven spans, giving it a distinctive look that earned it the nickname *Ponte Diavolo*, or Devil's Bridge. Interestingly, some art historians speculate that this bridge and its surrounding valley could be the backdrop for Leonardo da Vinci's Mona Lisa. The great artist may well have spent a good bit of time living and working in Bobbio; then again, it may be that Bobbio's publicity department has just been particularly effective in disseminating this notion.

Bobbio's Bridge and the Mona Lisa

A few art historians suggest that Bobbio's iconic bridge, the Ponte Gobbo, is depicted in the background of the Mona Lisa, over her left shoulder. Fueling this speculation is the number 72, which with great difficulty can be found in the painting under one of the bridge's spans; the original Roman-era bridge was badly damaged in the year 1472. It has been further claimed that the road over her right shoulder is the one traversing the hills of the Trebbia Valley at Bobbio. Anyone following this itinerary, though, will know that there are many such winding roads here.

Bobbio is famous for *maccheroni Bobbiese*, a pasta traditionally made with a knitting needle and served with beef *ragu*. A great place to find this is the **Albergo Ristorante Piacentino**, which faces the bustling Piazza San Francesco. The dining area here is extensive, and in good weather includes a meticulously manicured patio garden — beautiful, cool, and flowerful in season. The restaurant focuses on traditional Bobbiese cuisine, offering house-made pastas and a table-side prosciutto service, from which they plate up delicious meat cuts with flair. The garden included large amounts of basil and other herbs — it doesn't get fresher than that. Adventurous eaters will be delighted

to know that a traditional specialty of Bobbio is snails in various forms, including snail sausage.

Making sure we have a full tank of gas, we now set out on an even more wandering route, south and east along various river valleys extending from these precipitous Apennines. We pass through numerous tiny villages, any of which are good stops for a coffee or two; but finally we arrive at the impressive **Castello di Bardi**. As Rivalta is a fairytale castle with its distinctive princess tower, so Bardi is the archetypal foreboding fortress on the hill, imposing its dominance over the town below. The castle allows visitors remarkable access to its many spaces, including its towers and covered ramparts, and its dungeons and torture chambers complete with weapons and implements of "interrogation" on display. As Americans, we're not used to this kind of access in this sort of place without guides, guard rails, or liability waivers. Many unmarked little doors, narrow hallways, or cramped stairwells are open for exploration, so watch your step and keep track of your kids.

From Bardi, all the roads are twisty. Adventurous travelers may want to make their way north in search of the SP14. Just off of this highway stands the excavated remains of a small Roman outpost known as **Velleia Romana**. If these ruins seem like they're in some- one's backyard, that's because they are. Vestiges of ancient Rome like this are not u n c o m m o n throughout Italy, and they're fre- quently found

amid (relatively) modern homes and businesses. Velleia has a lot to see in its small space: the remnants of many Roman columns; the town's forum, baths, and other buildings; and a nearly 2000-year-old sign carved into the walls referring to "Imperial Caesar Vespasian".

Note: Confusingly (and typically), many of the roads in this neighborhood are marked as SP14, so look instead for the signs pointing the way to a "*Zona archeologica*", which is exactly what it sounds like.

From here we drive west, and come across the Val d'Arda. Having returned to the low farmlands, we follow the river route (SP47) north some 20 kilometers to the hilltop castle town of **Castell' Arquato**. It was built on the remnants of another Roman outpost that overlooked the river valley. The current castle, the **Rocca Viscontea** was built in the 14th century, and is one of the most impressive such structures we've seen. The view from the top of the castle tower surveys the valley in one direction, and the expansive town square in the other. The decorative swallow-tailed crenellations are characteristic of many castles in this region of Italy, and are now home to hundreds of actual swallows, as well as pigeons and crows.

Halfway between the upper castle and the lower town is the odd **Torrione Farnese**, a squat

tower that stands alone as a first line of defense for the castle proper. This tower is open only sporadically; it is operated by the local Scuola D'arme Gens Innominabilis, a club of medieval fencers and scholars who periodically perform demonstrations, duels, tournaments, and battle re-enactments in the town. Don't miss this if you're lucky enough to happen upon it when it's open. The tower is four stories tall; the floors are connected by one dizzying spiral staircase from the ground floor to the top platform.

There is food aplenty in Castell'Arquato, including two of our favorite restaurant destinations. **Ristorante Maps**, in the lower town right on the Piazza Europa, is an elegant restaurant with a secluded and romantic garden. The food is excellent, modern and upscale cuisine influenced by tradition. They offer two menus, *carta del terra* and *carta del mare* — from the land and from the sea. Diners can choose one, or mix them. Everything is perfectly prepared and

served with pride, from a refreshing and cool shrimp and fava bean appetizer, to delicate, savory crepes, to delicious handmade pasta with *ragu di cinghiale*. They also make a noteworthy *nocino*, a walnut liqueur typical to the region. Though we usually find this drink too sweet, theirs is perfect, packed with walnut flavor.

There is surprisingly little lodging in Castell' Arquato, but across the *piazza* from Ristorante Maps is **Hotel Leon d'Oro**. It offers a fairly upscale stay — and perhaps the softest beds in Italy — for a decent price. It includes a modest breakfast, but you're paying for the location. The rooms facing the piazza grant a bird's-eye perspective of modern nightlife in this ancient town.

Just off of this *piazza* we find **Gelateria del Borgo**. Though it looks like any other Italian gelato shop, this one is different. This is artisanal gelato, homemade with fresh, local ingredients like real IGP-certified hazelnuts from Piemonte, actual pistachios, and fresh fruit. If you only get one cup of gelato in your visit to Italy, get it at this place. Better yet, get two.

At the top of town, directly next to the castle on the Piazza del Municipio, is **Taverna delle Falconiere**. Be ready for an epic meal here: The gorgeous, flower-filled patio overlooking the castle is surpassed only by the graciousness of the hosts and the quality of the food. Chef Eros expertly prepares his dishes with great skill; his wife Margherita serves and talks to her guests in as many as five languages. They offer a great *pinzimonio* plate, a simple but delicious way to really experience the place you're visiting: Fresh, raw seasonal vegetables to be eaten with salted olive oil. Eros' pastas dishes are perfectly made, including an unexpected *risotto Milanese* seasoned with saffron. He also makes his own *amari* — the usual regional liqueurs, including *nocino* and *bargnolino* (another typical and popular *liquore* made from

the berries of a blackthorn plant). But if you ask for *qualcosa differente* ("something different"), Eros may treat you to samples of his other varieties: A delicious herbal *amaro*, and one he calls "*Rosolio*", made from thousands of rose petals and a few vanilla beans. You won't want to leave this place, and when you do you probably shouldn't drive until you've had a few *espressi*.

Leaving Castell'Arquato, we make our way south across the rolling hills and farmlands until we reach another hilltop fortification. We step back into time as we walk through the gate of the tiny **Castello di Vigoleno**, which at the time of this writing had 5 residents. Calling the place a "castle town" is in this case literal: The crenellated castle walls enclose the entire tiny village, which includes a couple of shops, a bar, and the Church of San Giorgio. And of course there's the keep of the castle itself, which has been converted into a high-end destination lodging and restaurant. Vigoleno is a popular location for weddings, and it's easy to see why — it is a setting right out of an epic medieval

romance. The hotel suites are lavish, as befits the stature of a 10th century ducal castle. They also offer smaller and simpler rooms in some of the adjacent town buildings, which make for a fantastic stay.

The shops within the castle bear mentioning: One specializes in *liquori* of dozens of varieties (made from dandelion, lavender, orange, and many other unusual ingredients) as well as wine from the region. The other has a few wines and *amari*, but also has chocolates, jams, pastas, meats and cheeses from various local producers. Both shops carry the artisanal products of one of our favorite liquor-makers, **Liquorificio Colombo**; if they're closed, it is advisable at some point to make the 25 minute drive to visit the spa town of **Salsomaggiore Terme** to find a bottle or two of Colombo's *Camomillina* liqueur. This elixir is our favorite of Colombo's many varieties of *amari* and *grappa*. Over the years many bottles have made their way to our liquor cabinet (with the help of our suitcases) and are now in demand by our dinner guests.

Colombo *Liquorificio*

It's always worth asking if there are any good locally made *amari* or *liquori*. In business since 1905, Colombo is a great example of the production of great *liquori* with traditional methods. In addition to their signature *Camomillina*, they offer several other traditional concoctions common to Emilia-Romagna: The syrupy sweet *nocino* is an extraction from unripe walnuts picked in June; medicinal and therapeutic *bargnolino* is made from berries of *prunus spinosa*, a locally-common thorny plant. Colombo also makes more exotic elixirs from *mele cotogne* (quince) and *tarassaco* (dandelion) among a rotating variety of others.

WHERE TO EAT

Rivalta

Locanda del Falco ★★★★ $$
DESTINATION RESTAURANT

Absolutely un-missable restaurant located within the walls of the Castle of Rivalta. On festivals the restaurant is lit entirely with candles, and in cooler months there is an open log fire. Reservations are highly recommended as this restaurant is very popular with locals and always crowded. Be sure to visit the very well-stocked *bottega* next door; if it's closed the staff at the restaurant will happily open it upon request so you can shop. Unusually, they have a large collection of Scottish whiskeys here also.

Closed Tuesdays.
http://www.locandadelfalco.com

Bobbio

Albergo Ristorante Piacentino ★★ $$

Don't be fooled by Piacentino's modest front — it boasts a lovely, lush garden area in the back lined with tables for al fresco dining. When making a reservation be sure to request one of those. This family owned restaurant specializes in local cuisine; try the "Maccheroni alla Bobbiese".

Closed Mondays.

http://www.hotelpiacentino.it

Castell'Arquato

Ristorante Maps ★★★ $$

Found in the 'basso' section of Castell'Arquato, very near Hotel Leon D'Oro. In warmer months there is a very nice outdoor sitting area designed around a working fountain. Patio is shaded by light awnings, beautifully lit up by candlelight. Interior dining room is cozy, warm; dozens of artworks by local artists adorning the walls. Food is upscale, inventive, beautifully presented.

Closed Mondays and Tuesdays.

http://www.ristorantemaps.com

Castell'Arquato

Gelateria del Borgo ★★ $

Unassuming little gelateria in the town 'basso' next door to Ristorante Maps which makes all their own gelato, using fresh fruit and DOP hazelnuts and pistachios. Grab a gelato (multiple flavors of course), then walk past Hotel Leon D'Oro to the large, beautiful town park and enjoy a lovely stroll.

Taverna delle Falconiere ★★★★ $$
DESTINATION RESTAURANT

At the top of town next door to the castle, one of the most beautiful outdoor dining areas we've ever seen, and that is saying a lot. Situated in between the castle and the Torrione Farnese, Falconiere's stunning patio is ringed with flower boxes dripping with geraniums; any way you look, you'll be rewarded with incredible views out its porticoes over the town below. Chef Eros makes everything in-house, including an ever-changing variety of after-dinner liqueurs. If he has any "Rosolio" (rose petal liqueur) be sure to try it. Reservations generally not necessary as the restaurant is fairly large, but if you want a corner table on the patio make sure to stop in and ask for one earlier in the day.

Closed Mondays.

http://www.tavernadelfalconiere.com/index.htm

Rivalta

Torre di San Martino ★★★ $$$

Torre di San Martino is located within the grounds of the Castle of Rivalta, but best of all, it's right next to the excellent restaurant Locanda del Falco. Rooms are fairly small but quite cozy, with four poster beds. Breakfast (continental) is served in a room on the second floor.

http://www.torredisanmartino.it

Castell'Arquato

Hotel Leon D'Oro ★★★ $$$

Leon D'Oro is located in the town's 'basso', and offers free parking right outside (with hanging tag provided by management). We recommend requesting one of the rooms on the top floor as those have the best views over the town. Continental breakfast is served on the ground floor. Rooms are modern, light and airy, and the puffy beds are some of the most comfortable we've found in Europe.

http://www.leondorocastellarquato.it/en/

Rivalta

Bottega attached to Locanda del Falco ★★★★ $

Very well stocked alimentari attached to Locanda del Falco. Produce, local meats and cheeses, artisanal chocolates and cakes, unusual liqueurs, plus a large collection of Scottish whiskeys. Worth a visit just for the smells, and to snap a photo. If the store is closed, the restaurant staff will be happy to open it when there is a break in service.

Salsomaggiore Terme

Liquorificio Colombo ★★★★ $

One of our favorite liqueur makers in Italy, with an incredible liqueur of chamomile that is the most-often requested liqueur at our home. Liqueurs of other flavors vary but can include orange, violet, lemon, walnut, and more. If the Liquorificio is closed (which is often the case), try the alimentari "Salso Formaggi", located on the same street, via Parma 58. Colombo liqueurs and candy may also be found in the castle shops at the castle of Vigoleno.

http://www.camomillinacolombo.it

Rivalta

Castle of Rivalta ★ ★ ★ $

Castle has many rooms open to visit, including dungeons, kitchens, bedrooms, the extensive Military Uniform museum, and a museum dedicated to the Battle of Lepanto. The Castle was a favorite destination of the British Royal family and their photos can be found in some of the rooms. Tours are guided and offered in Italian; however English tours (also tours in German and French) are available by request for an extra €50 (plus the €9/person entry fee). Do yourself a favor and pair a visit to the Castle with a lunch or dinner at the amazing restaurant Locanda del Falco.

Opening times vary by season and date, and can be found here:

http://www.castellodirivalta.it/joomla/

Bobbio

Basilica di San Colombano ★ ★ ★

15th century church, with a stunning, huge 12th century mosaic on a lower level near the crypt. In the crypt proper you can visit the chapel and resting place of St. Columbanus.

Open 8:00-7:00; festival days open 8:00-12:30 and 2:30-7:00.

Duomo of Santa Maria Assunta ★★★

11th century cathedral with blue painted vaulted ceilings that look like a nighttime sky full of stars.

Open 8:00-7:00; festival days open 8:00-12:30 and 2:30-7:00.

Ponte Gobbo (Devil's Bridge) ★★★★

Ancient bridge straddling the River Trebbia, purported to be the bridge pictured behind the Mona Lisa in Da Vinci's famous painting. Alternatively called the "Devil's Bridge" and the "Hunchbacked Bridge".

Bardi

Castle of Bardi ★★★ $

Enjoy a walk along the shops in Bardi's lower town streets on your way to this huge castle.

Adults €5.50, children 7-14 €3. Varying opening times throughout the year, which can be found here: http://www.castellodibardi.it

Velleia

Velleia Romana ★★★ $

Roman ruins in the middle of the Emilian countryside south of Castell'Arquato. Closed New Year's Day and Christmas Day. Open every other day 9:00am-one hour before sunset.

€2 entry.

Castell'Arquato

Rocca Viscontea ★★★ $

€4 entry for adults, €3 for children (ages 6-12) and seniors.

Open year round Saturdays, Sundays and festival days mornings and late afternoons (with a lunch break between 1:00-2:00). Hours vary by season, full list found here:
http://www.castellidelducato.it/castellidelducato/castello.asp?el=rocca-viscontea-di-castellarquato

Vigoleno

Castle of Vigoleno ★★★★ $

One of the most beautiful castles in Emilia. It's possible to visit the interior, but it's worth it to see the castle with or without going inside, it's always possible to walk the tiny walled city. 5 residents live here year-round. The interior is open on weekends and festivals, times vary per season, as do rates of entry depending on how much of the castle you want to visit, all info can be found here: http://www.castellidelducato.it/castellidelducato/castello.asp?el=mastio-e-borgo-di-vigoleno

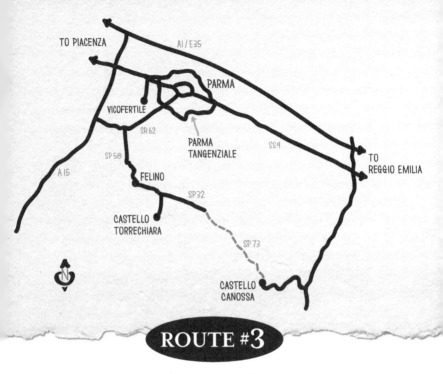

ROUTE #3

In and Around Parma

Prosciutto and Parmigiano

This route explores the source of some of Emilia-Romagna's most famous food. Dine in the castle that houses the Salami Museum; stay on a working cheese farm; learn about (and eat) prosciutto; and visit several medieval fortresses, including that of one of the most powerful women in European history.

Parma is one of those cities that by most tourist standards is considered a small town; and it is, compared to Rome or Milan. For us, it is very large, the kind of place that we usually avoid. In this case, though, we make a happy exception.

It would be enough that this is a hub of fine Emilia-Romagna food — the namesake of the famous *prosciutto di Parma* and the ubiquitous *parmigiano reggiano* cheese. But Parma also possesses a rich array of historical and cultural buildings and artwork. The city is bisected by the often-dry Parma River; most of the "good stuff" is on the east side, like their extensive National Gallery complex. This series of museums includes

an art gallery and an archaeological museum; various tickets are available for the different museum combinations, depending on your interest. One of the most impressive and unusual attractions here (and relatively unhampered by tourist crowds) is the **Teatro Farnese**. Also known as the "Wood Theater", this 1620s structure is made of incredibly ornately carved wood. The room exudes an aroma of lumber. The space is cavernous, with extremely steep stadium style benches for the audience. Don't miss the chance to go on stage or explore the backstage area, where assorteded ancient art and statuary are on display.

Finding our way through the streets to the nearby Piazza Duomo, we visit the **Duomo di Parma**, an incredible 12th-century Romanesque cathedral. This Duomo is an architectural marvel as well as an extensive art gallery in itself. Next to it is the relatively modest but fascinating **Baptistery**, a striking octagonal building of pink marble. Essentially an ornately decorated single room, the interior has twelve different arches, each containing art depicting various saints and biblical scenes. Carvings of religious icons are juxtaposed with pagan astrological figures; the architecture and placement of windows above the arches are designed to create sunlight effects on equinoxes and solstices as well as on certain holy days. Note

also the disturbing painting of Santa Lucia, patron saint of the blind, holding a plate with her own gouged-out eyes.

Prosciutto di Parma

What we call ham — meat made from the hind leg of a pig or a *cinghiale* (wild boar) — Italians call *prosciutto*. It is found *cotto* (cooked) or *crudo* (uncooked); both are delicious. The DOP variety made in the Parma region often has a faint but distinctive flavor of *parmigiano* cheese, as the pigs' diet includes whey by-products of the cheese-making process. These hams are produced through very specific processes, including salting the meat every day for a month before aging for as many as 16 months in carefully monitored conditions of temperature, humidity, and light.

One of the truly hidden gems in Parma is just off the Strada Melloni, close to the museum complex. Look for a little garden pathway off the street, which will lead you to the entrance of the **Camera di San Paolo**. This series of rooms belonged to a duchess of Piacenza, who commissioned the famous artist Corregio to paint the ceilings here. The resulting frescoes in two rooms are most fascinating examples of 16th century artwork. It feels like Coreggio is telling you stories and riddles over the centuries as you inspect these more closely. The frescoes include many "Grottesca", bizarre human-animal hybrids that can be seen occasionally when visiting these Renaissance sites

throughout the region. Different stories are depicted here, from arguing angels to hunting scenes to an inexplicable pair of disembodied feet. One fresco is ringed by several ram's heads; look closely and you'll notice that a couple of them are looking right at you, as if trying to let you in on the joke.

The term *grottesca*, it's worth noting, comes from artwork in Roman times that decorated walls and ceilings of a basement or cave ("grotto"), which were often depictions of fantastic, impossibly hybridized or misshapen characters. If someone today describes something as "grotesque", you might respond by saying "Oh, you mean it's reminiscent of Roman-era or

Renaissance cave paintings?" (Note: The authors are not responsible for one's consequent reputation as a snooty know-it-all.)

Just across the river from the museums is the large **Parco Ducale**, a lovely place for a walk to get away from the bustle of the streets. At the east end is the grand Ducal Palace. You can walk west for nearly a half mile through well-kept gardens, under ancient trees, and past sculpture displays to the other end to see the fish pool and its 18th-century Trianon Fountain.

The streets are full of shops of all kinds, like **Amata** handknit woolens. This tiny shop on a little side street has hand-knit sweaters, hats, gloves, scarves, and jackets. Their wares are not cheap, but that's to be expected where something is handmade. Their signature item is an unusual scarf/hat combination that covers your neck and head snugly.

All this walking works up an appetite. Fortunately, we're in the heart of a wonderful food culture, and great meals abound. For authentic and local fare, try **Ristorante Gallo d'Oro**, down a side alley just south of the large Piazza Garibaldi. Start with a local plate of *salumi misti* (mixed meats, including *prosciutto* but also *culatello* and several types of salami), which will probably be served with chunks of aged *parmigiano* and *torta fritta*, little hot pockets of fried bread. (Not to be confused

Parmigiano reggiano

Most Americans are familiar with "parmesan" cheese, knowing it as a bland, granular pizza or pasta condiment shaken out of a green canister. But the word is an Anglicized version of *parmigiano*, meaning "from Parma". The DOP-designated *parmigiano reggiano* cheese is made in the vicinity of the towns of Parma and Reggio Emilia, and is one of the most prized products of Emilia-Romagna. The nearly 90-pound wheels proudly bear the identifying stamp on their rinds. Don't throw out the rinds! It's all cheese, and pieces of the dried outer shell can be used to deliciously season soups and sauces.

with the inexplicably popular American "food" known as "Hot Pockets", which we do not recommend eating at any time.) Seasonally stuffed *tortelli* pasta are handmade, and usually covered with more delicious *parmigiano*. Meat dishes include house-made *salsiccia* (sausage) and a *stinco di maiale*, a chunk of roasted pork on the bone that looks like something a caveman would be eating at a fire, if he were an expert in herbs and seasoning. All of this goes down wonderfully with a bottle or two (or three) of the house *lambrusco*.

For a more upscale dining experience, head west out of the old *centro* on Via Gramsci and find **Ristorante Cocchi**, set in a modern brick building in the Hotel Daniel. The main dining room is filled with beautiful modern art, and has an elegant, light, and airy feeling. The  menu is a bit pricey but worth the experience; everything is of the highest quality, handmade and artistically presented, like their pumpkin souffle with cream of *parmigiano*. Some of the dishes are delivered with a show — for example, a polenta and meat dish for which they bring out a cart full of the roast meats and slice them to order as you watch. The wine list is more extensive and diverse than usual, offering oenophiles plenty to choose from. *Aperitivi* selections include either prosecco, Franciacorta, or champagne (served with *parmigiano* of course) for those who want to learn the finer points of these sparkling whites.

Parking in Parma is not difficult: The ring road outside the *centro* has a lot of inexpensive underground parking. You get a ticket upon entering, and empty spaces are marked with a green light. Make sure you bring your ticket with you. The garages have no attendants, so yo pay at a machine near the exits before returning to your car. Your paid ticket gets you out of the garage.

When we've had enough of Parma's big-city energy, we drive out of town to find some of the sources of this great food. In no time we're in the country, surrounded by farms. One such is a lodging as well as a dairy farm: **Agriturismo B&B Leoni**. Hosts Lola and Cinzia offer a nice accommodation and a homemade breakfast, and their little shop on-site sells *parmigiano* and *lambrusco* made on their premises. For around €14 you can bring home a 2-pound wedge of parmigiano that would cost 50 bucks in the States, making yourself the envy of Italophile foodies and cheapskates both.

Driving further south, we come to the small, unassuming town of Felino. Hidden in the hills on the outskirts of town is the grand 9th century **Castello di Felino**. Now privately owned and hired out for large events, Felino Castle is not generally open for tourists, with two exceptions. Its cellars house the **Museo di Salame di Felino**, which gives visitors a great history of the process of salami making in the region. *Salame di Felino* in particular is locally famous, noted in part for the peppercorns prominent in the ancient recipe. The museum is self-guided with information signs in Italian and English, and includes displays of the equipment used in the production, so visitors can see literally how the sausage is made.

The courtyard of the castle is also the entrance to the upscale and excellent restaurant **Locanda della Moiana**, which offers traditional local cuisine and wine in a polished and stylish atmosphere. The walls of the dining room are covered with artwork and historical documents, making it almost an extra museum visit as well as a fine dining experience. It should go without saying that this is the place to get a plate of *salame di Felino* — it doesn't get any more local than this.

Leaving Felino, we drive south to the municipality of Langhirano, where resides the **Museo del Prosciutto** (ham museum), for those who have not yet had their fill of deli history. However, before reaching Langhirano proper, we stop at the striking and well-preserved **Castello di Torrechiara**. Built in the 15th century, it sits on a hill, presiding over the landscape and its little town below. Its rooms contain all manner of historical artwork, including *grottesca* and other frescoes depicting chivalric scenes from medieval times. The wall decorations in the *Camera d'oro* (Golden Room) were once trimmed in actual gold, a testament to the wealth (and therefore the power) of the resident rulers of the time.

Inside the walls, just outside the castle proper, is the beautiful and excellent **Taverna del Castello**. Grab a drink in the cozy and cute cantina on the

first floor before your meal. The interior upstairs is warm and romantic, all brick and stone and timbers. If the weather allows, the patio is lovely; the view over the valley is stunning. The menu is relatively small, and that's a good thing; each dish is made with great care and quality. Enjoy a too-big order of *torta fritta* with local *prosciutto*, *parmigiano-reggiano* cheese and *aceto balsamico* (balsamic vinegar; more on this delicacy in our next itinerary). The pastas are all handmade here, and vary depending on the time of year; their beautiful *ravioli* are stuffed with different local seasonal ingredients.

After sating our hunger for history and cuisine (at least for now), we take another meandering route south and east through the beautiful farmland from where so much of this great food comes. We cross the Parma River and then the Enza River. We make out a small, ghostly silhouette of a ruined castle on the horizon, atop a bleak, rocky outcropping that overlooks the Val d'Enza. This is the **Rocca di Canossa**, a 10th century castle that was the ancestral seat of Matilda di Toscana. Matilda was a powerful noblewoman of the 11th century known for her military prowess and diplomatic accomplishments, including subduing King Henry IV in 1077 during his conflict with Pope Gregory VII.

Parking is found at the foot of the hill, next to a small restaurant and bar — a coffee before hiking to the castle is advisable. The walk up is steep but not far, and rewards us with great views of the countryside, including the sites of other distant hilltop castles. From here it is easy to see how Matilda was able to successfully control this valley for so many decades. A small museum

Matilda of Canossa

Heiress to a great kingdom in Tuscany, a 9-year-old Matilda and her mother were captured by invading Germanic forces led by Emperor Henry III in 1055. When she was liberated to her ancestral lands a year later, she became a well-read student of history, politics, and languages. Her knowledge served her well when her husband died, leaving her in charge of her family's vast kingdom. She was very religious, and a steadfast supporter of Pope Gregory VII. When Henry IV threatened Italy in 1077, Matilda led her army to defeat him and accept his surrender at her Canossa Castle.

offers a good bit of information about Matilda, the castle, and their history. Exploring the ancient stone remnants of this thousand-year-old fortification, it's easy to imagine the centuries of lives and events that led from stark medieval sites like this to the riches of the Renaissance that can be seen throughout this region.

Vicofertile

Agriturismo B&B Leoni ★★ $$

Very rural retreat on a farm in the Emilian countryside, on a working Parmigiano Reggiano cheese farm. You're on a farm, so you'll hear cows lowing, but at night it's very peaceful and it's quite close to Parma. Breakfast is served in the breakfast room on the ground floor and frequently offers cakes or tortes made by hosts Lola and Cinzia. There is also a small shop on site where you can buy cheese and wine made on the farm itself.

http://www.agriturismoleoni.com

Parma

Cocchi ★★★ $$$

Upscale, popular restaurant located within the Hotel Daniel on the outskirts of the old town. Parking can easily be found in the residential neighborhood nearby if none is available at the hotel. Reservations are a must as this place is very well known and always busy, even in the off season. Bright, airy restaurant serving exquisite food, with walls covered in art by local artists.

Closed Saturdays.
http://www.ristorantecocchi.it

Felino

Castle of Felino: Locanda della Moiana ★★★★ $$

Located within the privately owned Castle of Felino, the Locanda serves excellent, seasonal food in the traditional style of the area. Service is friendly and welcoming, atmosphere is charming and serene. Be sure to get a plate of the salami di Felino, which is of course the specialty of the tiny town.

Though the Castle is closed to the public, the grounds are beautiful and we advise arriving early so you can take a leisurely walk around the castle before lunch.

Closed Mondays and Tuesdays.
http://locandadellamoiana.it

Torrechiara

Taverna del Castello ★★★★ $$

Popular with the locals, the Taverna is located within the walls of the Castle of Torrechiara. In warmer months there is a lovely patio to sit on; in cooler months you retreat to the cozy dining rooms. Plan a visit to the Castle either before or after your meal as it's one of the best castles in Emilia. Reservations are a good idea as the restaurant can frequently be full.

Open every day for lunch and dinner.
http://www.tavernadelcastello.it

Vicofertile

Shop at Agriturismo B&B Leoni

Tiny shop on the grounds of B&B Leoni, which is itself located on a working dairy farm. It's possible to buy Parmigiano Reggiano all over Italy, but if you want to buy directly from a farm that makes it this is a great option. Huge wedges of already-vacuum-packed Parmigiano are on offer, of varying ages: 18 months, 24 months and 36 months. The farm also sells its own (unlabeled) lambrusco.

If the store is closed during opening hours, just

ring the bell by the door and someone will happily come out to open up, often either owner Lola or Cinzia.

Closed Monday and Sunday afternoons. Open mornings from 9:00-12:30 and 5:00-6:30.

http://www.agriturismoleoni.com

Parma

Amata Handknit Wools ★★ $$$
Small shop in the old town of Parma selling hand knit wool scarves, hats, gloves, sweaters, wraps and more made by the owner. Many of the designs are created by the owner and quite unusual.

Via Nazario Sauro 7/A .

Closed Sundays. Open Monday-Saturday 9:30-12:30 and 4:30-7:30.

WHAT TO SEE

Felino

Castle of Felino: Salame Museum ★★ $
The Museum of Salame is located on the lower floor of the Castle of Felino, and makes an interesting and fun stop before taking lunch at the Locanda della Moiana upstairs. The museum has a few rooms illustrating the history of salame and how it is made, culminating in a video in the last room. Video and

signs are in Italian but English guides are available.

5€ entry, reduced rates for large groups and children.

Closed December-February, Open weekends, times vary and can be found here: http://www.musei-delcibo.it/Ing/page.asp?IDCategoria=1262&IDSezione =7926

Parma

Duomo ★★★

This 12th-century Romanesque cathedral is a staggering sight, inside and out.

Free to enter. Open 9:00-12:30 and 3:00-7:00 every day.

Baptistery ★★★ $

The pink marble of the Baptistery is best viewed at sunset, but it is striking at any time of day.

6€ to enter, 4€ for students with ID and seniors. Open 9:00-12:30 and 3:00-6:30.

Teatro Farnese and National Gallery ★★★ $

Admission to both, 6€; after 2pm, only 3€. 18-25 year-olds, admission 3€; after 2pm, 1.5€. To see just the Teatro, admission 2€; 18-25 year-olds, 1€. Under 18, free entrance.

Free admission to all on the first Sunday of every month.

http://www.parmabeniartistici.beniculturali.it/en

Camera di San Paolo ★★★★ $

One of the most overlooked but most memorable sights in the Emilia. Gorgeous, sometimes funny murals by the famous artist Coreggio.

Closed Monday, January 1, May 1, December 25. Open Tuesday-Sunday 8:30-2:00. 2€ entry.

http://www.parmabeniartistici.beniculturali.it/al tri-luoghi/en/camera-di-san-paolo/orari-e-accesso-alla-camera/

Canossa

Rocca di Canossa ★★ $

Admission 3€.

The seat of power of Matilda of Tuscany in the 11th century, this castle is now ironically in ruins, but worth a visit for its views and its evocative setting.

Closed Mondays in summer and Mondays and Tuesdays the rest of the year; open mornings and late afternoons. Closed on some holidays, full listings here: http://castellodicanossa.it/museo/orari.html

Langhirano

Prosciutto Museum ★★ $

Exactly what it sounds like.

Closed December-February. Open Saturday, Sunday and festivals 10:00-6:00. Open Monday-Thursday by group appointment only. 4€ entry.

http://www.museidelcibo.it/prosciutto.asp

Torrechiara

Castle of Torrechiara ★ ★ ★ $

Very beautiful castle in the Emilian countryside perched on a steep hill that dominates the farmland below. Good site to pair with the Camera di San Paolo in Parma, notice the similarities in the bizarre 'grottesca' murals. On site is the excellent restaurant Taverna del Castello.

Closed Mondays. November-February, open Tuesday-Friday 9:00-4:30; Saturday, Sunday and festival days 10:00-5:00. From March-October, open Tuesday, Sunday and festivals 10:30-7:30; and Wednesday-Saturday 8:30-7:30. 3€ entry. Free entrance every first Sunday of the month.

http://www.castellideducato.it/castellideducato/castello.asp?el=castello-di-torrechiara

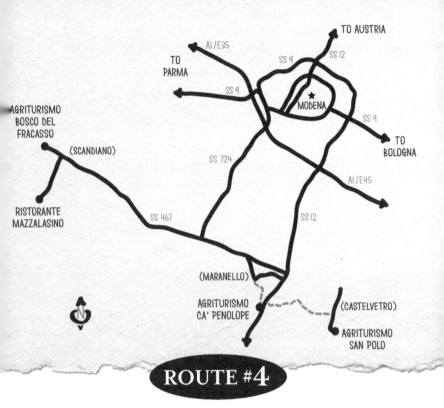

ROUTE #4

In and Around Modena

Architecture and *Aceto*

On this route, we will eat and sleep at working farms in the heartland; dine with the locals at a popular restaurant whose portion sizes defy belief; stroll around one of the biggest town squares in Europe; and visit the workshop of a glass artist who was trained in Venice.

71

Aceto balsamico di Modena is the most prized balsamic vinegar in the world, and in this region it is
very highly valued but also commonplace. The city
of Modena is smaller than Parma but still fairly
large by our standards; nevertheless, its far-reach-
ing history, staggering architecture, and rich food
culture make it a great stop in our exploration of
Emilia-Romagna. Before we delve into the city,
though, there are a few spots worth visiting in the
Modenese countryside. After all, we are still in this
lush breadbasket region; we owe it to ourselves,
and our palates, to explore the sources of some of
this great food.

Balsamic vinegar

Like "parm cheese", "balsamic vinaigrette" is a typical condiment
on American dining tables. But true balsamic vinegar (*aceto balsamico*)
comes from Modena or Reggio Emilia, and is designated with the DOP
label. (The less rarified but still fine type of Modenese balsamic vinegar
is labeled IGP — see Route 1.) The most highly regarded (except in
Reggio) is *Aceto Balsamico Tradizionale di Modena*, and is made only in
Modena province, from particular grapes, using specified processes
and bottling. It is aged in wooden barrels for at least twelve and sometimes 18 or 25 or even 100 years.

To the west and south of Modena is the sprawl-
ing industrial town of Scandiano. Fighting our way
through its traffic brings us abruptly back to the
farmlands, where we find the **Agriturismo Bosco**

del Fracasso. Anna Brevini and her husband
Maurizio run this farm, raising various livestock,
growing grapes for *lambrusco* and other vegetables
and fruit, and producing delicious jams, honeys,
and salsas. The guest lodging is modest but immac-
ulate. Breakfast is a delicious assortment of Anna's
homemade baked goodies, along with *parmigiano*

cheese and Anna's jams. When we asked *"Che bere è normale?"* ("What's normal to drink?") for breakfast, she poured two glasses from a half-full bottle: *"Prosecco della ieri sera..."* — last night's prosecco. That's farm life. For a modest fee, if arranged ahead of time, Anna will cook dinner for her guests as well.

The Brevini's place is certified by the consortium of *"Fattorie Didattiche"*, an "educational farm" that offers classes and activities for kids and adults in the summertime. Visitors can learn how the products are made, experience how the farm operates, and even meet the animals. Depending on the timing, Anna might also arrange a tour of the nearby *parmigiano* producer — their storeroom, with floor-to-ceiling shelves full of aging cheese wheels (each about 86 pounds), is as striking as any medieval abbey.

The term *"bosco del fracasso"* literally means "fight in the woods". The area saw a great deal of combat over the centuries in medieval times, being on the road between Modena and the much-embattled castle of Canossa (see Route #3) to the west.

A mere ten-minute drive to the south of Bosco del Fracasso is one of the best examples of *cucina Emiliana* and one of our most memorable food destinations. About 1 kilometer past the tiny hamlet of Iano on the SP7 is the modest roadside **Ristorante Mazzalasino**. The place has no menus — one of the *camerieri* (servers) will come to the table and tell you what they have that day. Huge *antipasti* plates go to each table — see our Introduction for our funny first experience with this "deli tray". Next follows a trio of different pastas, all freshly made minutes earlier, and all delicious. If somehow you're not totally stuffed at this point, several meat dishes are available, sometimes including freshly caught game from the nearby woods. The restaurant is always full of local, working-class folks; eating at Mazzalasino is the closest most of us will get to eating in an Italian grandma's kitchen.

After all this traipsing over the *colline, torrenti, e bosco* (hills, streams, and woods), we're ready to brace for some big city excitement — and by "big city", we mean a town with a population of less than 200,000. Situated between the Panaro and Secchia Rivers, ancient **Modena** used to be criss-crossed by canals like an inland Venice, making it easily accessible to boat travelers and merchants. "Mutina splendidissima" (so called by none other than Cicero) was already a thriving center of commerce in Roman times, and therefore strategically vital to the region. Consequently it endured multiple invasions, sieges, sackings, and floodwaters, the last of which drove people out of the city for some 200 years. When the waters receded, this prime real estate led to a rebirth of the city in the 9th century, and it grew and prospered from then on.

Today the canals (and the flood waters) are gone, but several of the streets are affectionately named (like the central *Corso Canalgrande*) in recognition of their ancestral waterways. It is a colorful city, literally as well as figuratively; many of the building rows are painted with festive rainbow hues rather than the usual oranges, tans, and yellows. Modena's commerce, too, is still as vibrant as ever. One of the most fun places to visit here is the famous **Mercato Albinelli**, an open-air market

with dozens of stalls where local food vendors and artisans ply their wares. Wandering the aisles of this bustling bazaar provides a sweeping tour of regional foodstuffs, from fresh produce to local meats and cheeses to baked goods to oil, vinegar, salt and spices. Don't miss stall #94, a baker selling a traditional  cookie called "*amaretti*" — chewy, sweet *biscotti* infused with almond essence. The smells are tantalizing; the temptation to try a bit of everything risks compromising your appetite for lunch. As always when eating in Emilia Romagna, pace yourself.

In the 11th century Modena was under control of the aforementioned countess Matilda (see Route #3), who may well have had a hand in commissioning some of the great buildings that stand magnificently today. Foremost of these became Modena's **Piazza Grande**, a UNESCO World Heritage site. The huge open town square is flanked

by the imposing **Duomo** (the cathedral, one of the biggest in Italy) and its adjacent clock tower, the **Torre Ghirlandina**. The Duomo has some interesting statuary on its roof — note the unusual her-

maphroditic figure sitting with legs fully spread.

Some welcome shade can be found between the cathedral and the tower. The cool stone Porta

della Pescheria doorway is ornately carved with Zodiac-like calendar figures, Biblical depictions, Arthurian characters, and other fantastical scenes. We hear the sound of the bells tolling in the tower; they mingle with the voices of the congregation singing while taking communion inside the cathedral. This is one of those experiences that feel like a step back in time; indeed, the bells themselves are over 700 years old.

Tucked away in one corner of the Grand Piazza is a huge marble stone: This is the "Preda Ringadora", and was used alternatively as a speaking platform and a place to publicly punish and humiliate wrongdoers.

A couple of blocks north from the Tower, we stumble upon **La Gioja**, the shop of glass artist Susanna Martini. Susanna was trained by the traditional glass masters of Murano in Venice; she has applied her skills to creating a more modern art form. Glass jewelry is her specialty, and each piece is unique. One of her best selling and simplest pieces is "*una goccia di aceto*", a

drop of balsamic vinegar — her homage to Modena's life-blood, captured in glass as if frozen in mid-pour. Susanna's studio is right in the store, so if you are lucky you'll be able to watch her in

Monastic shops

Travelers in Italy can find monastic shops all over Italy, like the one at Modena's Church of Saint Peter and its Benedictine Monastery. Centuries of self-imposed isolation have led monks over the ages to establish and perfect agriculture, medical knowledge, and culinary craft: They are master makers of countless types of soaps, perfumes, medicinal tinctures and oils, honeys and jams, *liquori*, vinegar, olive oil, beer, wine, and more. Most active monasteries (or abbeys, or friaries) have a small store where are sold monastic products from all over Europe as well as their own in-house goods.

action, creating these pieces of art before your eyes.

In the south part of Modena's *centro*, we find the **Chiesa di San Pietro** (Church of Saint Peter) and the adjacent **Monastero dei Benedettini** (Benedictine Monastery). After a walk through Modena's narrow little streets, walking inside directly into this cavernous, cool space is a welcome change of pace. The church's unusual art and architecture includes several depictions of fantasy figures like satyrs and giant seahorses. The monastic shop next door, **Spezieria Monastica**, sells products made by Benedictine monks: wine, beer, *liquori*, teas, honeys and jams, herbal perfumes, soaps, tinctures, and candies. Just past this shop is an entrance to the local monks' gardens, where they grow the stuff that they use to make their goods (as well as their dinners).

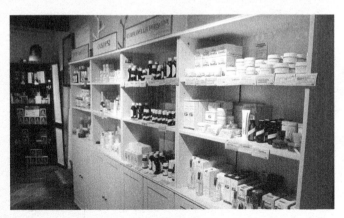

Modena's circling ring road has easy and cheap pay-and-display parking spaces, and parking there is free during lunchtime hours — a testament to the city's priorities in eating well. Our favorite restaurant is **Trattoria Il Fantino**, a very casual place filled with locals, tucked away down a little side street a couple of blocks from the Grand Piazza. There are only a few dishes available at any given time. Everything is handmade and of a very high quality, served in a light and cheery atmosphere. The walls are filled with food- and wine-themed art, whetting diners' appetites while their dishes are made from scratch: A simple plate of *tortelloni* with butter and sage, delicate but rich; wine-

soaked, falling-of-the-bone pork ribs; a very artistic dessert, *sfogliatelle* ("pages" of crispy, flaky pastry) stacked with fresh sweet whipped cream in between and topped

with a liqueur-soaked cherry.

For lodging we escape the big city and head out to the countryside. About a half-hour south of Modena is Maranello, a small, relatively modern town. Just on the southern outskirts is **Ca' Penelope**, a restored organic farm that sells its products (*marmellate*, *olio*, *lambrusco*, and even eggs and vegetables) and offers comfortable rooms and

Borlengo and Torta Fritta

In Italy, bread is served with every meal, but each region has its specialty. In the Parma area, *torta fritta* is the popular "hot pocket" bread — delicate, fried puffs of bread often served with *parmigiano* and *prosciutto*.

The word *burla* — a prank or joke — is the root of the *borlengo*, typical in the Modena area. These are extremely thin sheets of bread, cooked in a greased iron pan, then seasoned. One legend has it that a stingy innkeeper served bread made from watered-down dough, but the result was so popular that guests returned to him again and again — the joke was on him.

breakfast to travelers looking for a relaxed setting. It is indeed very peaceful — until the *galli* (roosters) start crowing at 4:00 AM or so — one of them sounds for all the world like he's yelling "*WHAT... the Hellllll!*" Since they're Italian roosters, and probably not fluent in English, we don't take it personally.

Ca' Penelope offers excellent homemade dinners (no menus, just whatever they've prepared that day from the farm), but only on weekends and with a reservation. It's important to remember that this is, first and foremost, a working farm. The food is rustic and delicious, and most of it comes directly from the farm. We also find great farm-

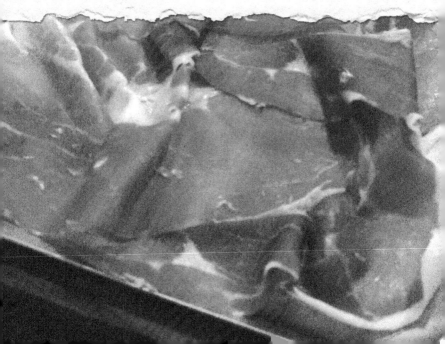

to-table fare in the nearby village of Castelvetro to the east. After a twisting 20-minute drive from Ca' Penelope, we arrive just south of Castelvetro across the Guerro River, and we're rewarded with a meal at the wonderful **Azienda Agricola San Polo**. They offer rooms here as well, but the real experience is the meal. Again, there are no menus. Plate after plate of food is brought in abundance, all produced locally. They also make their own wine here — *lambrusco* and *trebbiolo* (sparkling white). Diners here are swept up in a culinary adventure. You'll never know what's coming next; the only certainty is that everything is delicious, and the "food-miles" count is virtually nil. Friday and Saturday nights feature "Borlenghi", a paper-thin, multi-layer bread served piping hot from the wood oven, meant to be stuffed with *salumi* and cheese at the table. Of special interest is the bowl of local nuts, still in their shells. The bowl comes with a slate slab and a rock — yes, a rock. When in Emilia, do as the *Emilianese* do: Use the rock to crack the nuts on the slate. (Before you ask: Yes, the rock is locally sourced as well.)

Modena is the traditional home of Ferrari, Lamborghini, Maserati, and several other high-end car makers — the Ferrari Museum is in Maranello. If fast cars are your interest, this is a great place for you — but that's a different kind of driving itinerary. We're more interested in food, so we head to the relatively modern suburb of Spilamberto, the location of the **Museo dell'aceto balsamico tradizionale**, where we can learn all about how this precious and delicious liquid is made. The nearby **Antiquarium Museo Archeologico** offers some history of the area as well, and a glimpse of how the province of Modena evolved from a remote backwater in ancient times, to a commercial hub in the Roman era, to the bastion of culture that it became in the Renaissance, and finally to one of the capitals of Italian cuisine that it is today.

Scandiano

Agriturismo Bosco del Fracasso ★★ $$

Very rural retreat on a farm in the Emilian countryside. Hostess Anna Brevini, who speaks great English, lives and cooks on this idyllic working farm. Breakfast is served in the common room downstairs and features cakes, breads and tortes made by Anna. Anna also makes jams, compotes, and salsas that are available for purchase. During the day you'll hear the farm animals cooing and clucking; at night it's perfectly still and the sky is replete with stars.

http://www.boscodelfracasso.it

Maranello

Ca Penelope ★★★ $$

Another rural farm stay, this one near the small town of Maranello. On weekends the family that owns the B&B opens their country kitchen to cook dinner for guests, at a cost of 25€/person not including wine. Reservations for dinner are a must as they only open the kitchen if there are enough guests. Dinner is sourced mainly from ingredients from their farm and is well worth the experience. Breakfast is also delicious and can be requested for a small extra fee. Honeys, jams and other farm products can be purchased to bring home — don't miss the raspberry honey.

http://www.capenelope.it

WHERE TO EAT

Mazzalasino

Ristorante Mazzalasino ★★★ $

Casual restaurant always filled with locals serving traditional cuisine of the region. No muss, no fuss, just exactly the way their 'nonna' makes it. No menus, the waiter just gives you a few options of what the kitchen made that day, and you choose.

Closed Tuesday and Wednesday.

http://www.ristorantemazzalasinoscandiano.it

Modena

Trattoria Il Fantino ★★★★ $$

Tucked down a small side street in Modena you'll find the unassuming-looking little restaurant Il Fantino, which is a local favorite. No tourists here, just hungry Modenese eating delicious, handmade food. Excellent desserts.

Closed Sunday night and Mondays.
http://www.trattoriailfantino.it

Castelvetro

Azienda Agricola San Polo ★★★★ $$ (also shop)

Fantastic restaurant located on a farm, serving fresh seasonal food sourced from their farm. Menu changes monthly to reflect the changes of the seasons. Weekend nights they also feature 'borlenghi', a paper-thin, multi-layered bread cooked in a wood oven, served piping hot and meant to be stuffed with meats and cheeses by hand. Reservations a must.

Open for dinner Thursday, Friday and Saturday nights. Sunday and festivals, open for lunch and dinner. Friday and Saturday nights, borlenghi also available.

http://www.agrisanpolo.it

Modena

Mercato Albinelli ★★★★ $

Famous indoor market with hundreds of stalls selling fresh produce, meats, cheeses, baked goods, fresh flowers, and every other kind of foodstuff imaginable. Come here just for the smells and sights.

Closed Sunday. Open Monday-Friday 9:00am-2:30pm and Saturday 9:00-am-7:30pm.

http://www.mercatoalbinelli.it

La Gioja Glass Jewelry ★★★★ $$$

Glass artist Susanna Martini's stellar shop selling glass jewelry, vases, plates, even shoes Susanna had made by hand in the store in the small workshop there. Susanna is very creative and has created some very inventive and memorable pieces; you can often watch her creating the masterworks on site.

Closed Sunday and Monday. Open Tuesday-Friday 10:00-12:30 and 3:30-7:30. Open Saturday 10:00-7:30.

http://www.lagioja.com

Chiesa di San Pietro: Spezieria Monastica ★★★ $

Extensive monastic shop selling perfume, oil, soaps, creams, tinctures, candy, teas, liqueurs, jams and more made by the monks.

Closed Sunday morning. Open Monday-Sunday 9:30-12:30 and 3:30-7:30.

http://www.monasteromodena.it/attivita/spezieria.html

WHAT TO SEE

Modena

Chiesa di San Pietro ★★

Open 5:15-12:00 and 3:00-7:45.

Torre Ghirlandina ★★★ $

Modena's structural icon, Torre Ghirlandina dominates the main piazza. If the Tower is closed, stop by to hear noontime bells, which have been ringing since the 14th century.

Closed November-March, August, and Easter Sunday. Open Saturdays, Sundays and festival days between April-October. From 9:30-12:30 and 3:00-7:00. Also open January 31.

Duomo ★★★

Closed Mondays. Open Tuesday-Sunday 9:30-12:30 and 3:30-6:30.

Spilamberto

Balsamic Vinegar Museum

Entry: 2€, or 4€ with tasting.

Closed Mondays. Also closed December 25-26, January 1, Easter Sunday and August 15.

http://www.museodelbalsamicotradizionale.org

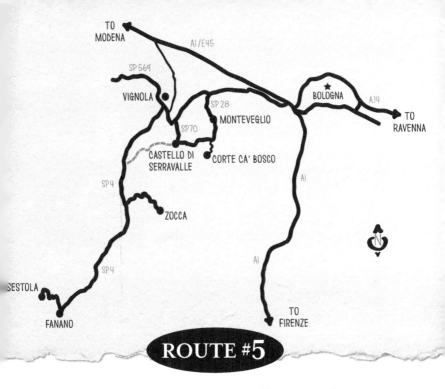

The Panaro River Valley and the Apennine Foothills

On this route we freely wander through a medieval fortress; sample a famous chocolate cake; marvel at an assortment of mechanical instruments housed in a mile-high castle; dine as a guest of a locally famous grill-master; and visit the hometown of the founder of Fairbanks, Alaska.

The Panaro is one of the two rivers (*"fiume"*) that flank Modena; it flows from several streams in the Apennines and makes its way north to the Po. Over the centuries, it gave rise to many market centers, one of which is the small but bustling town of Vignola, between Bologna and Modena. The town is dominated by the

huge 12th-century **Rocca di Vignola**. This medieval fortress historically stood watch over this important trade route from its position at one of the only crossings of the Panaro for many miles. Today it is one of Italy's most stunning, interesting, and fun castles to visit. Owned by a bank and operated by a historical foundation, it is totally free to enter.

Access to the castle rooms, towers, and dungeons is generally unrestricted and totally unguided, giving visitors free reign to explore everything this remarkable site has to offer. As in many castles, there are displays of medieval weaponry, and furniture and artwork from throughout the ages. Several huge rooms are adorned with what looks like an early version of wallpaper. This is actually finely detailed frescowork depicting various animals, resulting in names like the "Lion and Leopard Room" or the

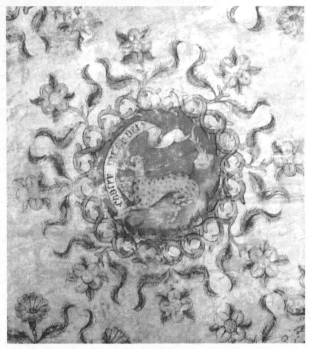

"Hound Room". In the upper stories of the fortress, a couple of the vertigo-inducing towers are open to climb freely, all the way to the topmost levels overlooking the entire town and river valley. Those who aren't claustrophobic can also descend some extremely steep and narrow stone stairways to visit the dank and ominous prison rooms. All together we need at least a couple of hours to really see everything and explore every fascinating room and alcove.

Vignola Cherry Festivals

Cherries from the hillsides around the castle town of Vignola carry the IGP designation; they are highly prized, and are considered to be among *i migliore* — the best — in Italy. The town celebrates its characteristic fruit with not one but two festivals: In late March/early May is the *Festa dei Ciliegi in Fiore*, the Cherry Blossom Festival, which is a medieval fair with a myriad of activities, including the building and parading of flower floats. In June, when the fruit are ripe, Vignola holds its *Tempo di Ciliege* ("Time for Cherries") fair, a celebration of all things gastronomic.

Just a few steps from the castle entrance is the famous **Caffé-Pasticceria Gollini**, a bakery that has been in the same family for generations. Their baked goodies are made by hand and with all-natural ingredients; they are most well-known for their *Torta Barozzi*, a flourless chocolate cake made with liqueur and coffee. This century-old secret family recipe is a work of culinary architecture, and is in fact named for 16th-century Vignola resident and architect Giacomo Barozzi. This cafe is a perfect end to a stroll through the incredible architecture of the castle.

Speaking of architecture: Not far from Vignola are two old medieval villages. One is **Castello di Serravalle**, a 13th-century fortified *borgo* that only takes a few minutes to walk through. Its strategic hilltop position was the point of much contention between Modena and Bologna during medieval times. (Eventually Bologna won.) Its fortress and tower are still intact; it has two small churches and a single restaurant, Taverna del Borgo. Of greater interest, though, is the **Ecomuseo della collina e del vino**, a museum that highlights, demonstrates, and preserves the culture, the agriculture, and the general way of life in this beautiful countryside.

This is also a starting point for many excursions by bike, horseback, and foot. Hiking and horse trails connect Serravalle with a large regional park to the northeast, at the edge of which is another medieval walled hilltop village and its ancient **Abbazia di Monteveglio**. (This is reachable by car as well, via the town of Monteveglio Capoluogo.) This village was another that came under the control of the famous Matilda of Canossa (see Route #3), who established the abbey and its Romanesque **Chiesa di Santa Maria Assunta** here in the 11th century. The **Torre del Castello** is the only intact part of the old fortress, and is open to visitors. There is a restaurant within these old town walls as well, **Trattoria del Borgo**. (The Italians are famously creative in many ways, but naming their restaurants is not necessarily one of those.)

The best place to eat in the area, though, and also the best place to stay, is about halfway between these two villages, at the rustic and beautiful **Corte di Ca' Bosco**. On a hillside overlooking the various farms and groves below, it offers clean and comfortable rooms at a good price; the real attraction here, however, is the restaurant. Many of the diners are locals; others have driven nearly an hour, from Modena and Bologna, to eat on the restaurant's beautiful *terrazza*. Owner Mirella makes delicious fresh *tortelli* and other pastas daily; her husband Andrea is locally famous as Ringo, "*DJ della griglia*" — "DJ of the grill". His meat dishes — local beef, sausage, chicken, and veal — are all cooked perfectly and with flair on an open-air wood grill. Another of Ringo's specialties is the "*piada*". As we travel farther east in this region, we approach the Romagna part of Emilia-Romagna, where a typical bread is the *piada*, a flour flatbread that looks a little like a tortilla. Slices of this are often included in the ubiquitous basket of bread

 at restaurants in eastern ER. We're still a bit west of Bologna — east of which is the Reno River and the edge of Romagna — but borders are porous, and happily so for food traditions. Ringo takes a whole *piada*, folds it in half, fills it with fresh ingredients (cheese or grilled vegetables or *prosciutto* or the like), and then

grills it alongside the meats, creating a delicious hot packet of local flavor. The grill smoke and cooking meat creates a light haze of tantalizing aroma that lingers throughout the evening. While he's cooking everyone's dinner, Ringo chats freely and jovially with his guests; the atmosphere is less like a restaurant and more like a barbecue at an old friend's house. The wine selections are plentiful, from local *lambrusco* to high-end imports (and in ER, *Chianti* is considered an import).

Assuming we manage to pull ourselves away from Mirella and Ringo's beautiful and comfortable place, we set out for a long drive into the wilderness. We return to the Fiume Panaro and follow the valley south towards its source in the Apennine foothills. This whole forested region is part of the *fascia della civiltá del castagno*, the "chestnut civilization zone". Chestnuts from the area are numerous and of high quality, and have been a vital part of the region's food culture for centuries; many dishes will include them, including salads, soups, desserts, even *liquori*.

The river leads us to the small ski resort town of **Fanano**, near Monte Cimone. The town's most notable church is the **Chiesa di San Silvestro**, down one of the little side streets. Founded as a monastery in the 8th century by Saint Anselmo, the site was a waypoint for religious pilgrims traversing the Apennines between Rome and Bologna. The current church was built in the 1200s, but then massively renovated in the 1600s to rotate its orientation 180 degrees. Consequently,

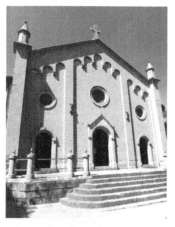 the remains of the ancient crypt (which would normally be under the altar) can be seen near the entrance. The vaulted ceilings are decorated with extensive frescoes, and the stations of the cross are depicted in bas-relief carvings. Some of the pillars are adorned by interesting carvings, depicting animals and otherworldly creatures alongside the more standard religious icons carved and painted throughout. There is a beautiful fresco of Saint Posidonia, the patron saint of Fanano, holding a cat-o-nine-tails. (Posidonia was killed by whipping.) His remains are in one of the small chapels of the church.

Another interesting note: Fanano is a sister city to Fairbanks, of all places. Local son Felice Pedroni, known in the U.S. as Felix Pedro, led American travelers to establish the Alaska town when he discovered gold there in 1901.

Driving through Fanano and following the winding SP324 road in the shadow of Monte Cimone brings us to another mountain town, **Sestola**. This is not somewhere we'd recommend going in the winter, as it is humming with people during the ski season; likewise, summertime is crowded with visitors on vacation. At all times of year it is also a destination for pilgrims and mystics. Nevertheless, in the spring or autumn, this is a wonderful place to visit. The lower village, which has a distinct Alpine feel, is a pedestrian-only zone (mostly), filled with shops, bars, and restaurants; keeping watch over the town from a nearby hill is the impressive **Castello di Sestola**, separated from

the lower town by a short but challenging footpath through the woods.

The current castle walls and structures date from the late 1500s, though the site was a military stronghold for some 800 years prior. Like many such castle sites in the region, this strategic location was historically much fought-over by the conflicting forces of Modena and Bologna. The castle now houses several museum installations. The fascinating **Museum of Mechanical Musical Instruments** displays dozens of old musical devices from the 17th century onward, from chiming clocks to cranking music boxes to miniature automated pianolas. Demonstrations of these instruments are scheduled periodically throughout the day. The **Museum of Mountain Civilization** contains tools, machinery, and other artifacts from ages past, giving an idea of what life was like in these highlands hundreds of years ago. An entire room is devoted to Teresina Burchi, a Sestola native who became a hugely successful opera star in the early 20th century. On display are photos and many items from the costumes she wore in

famous opera roles in Milan and elsewhere, and recordings of her singing are played all day long. Just wandering the buildings and grounds, though, is the best part of this visit, especially the scary but rewarding climb to the top of the big guard tower that commands a 360-degree view of Monte Cimone and the entire area. This

tower is only for the sure-footed and well-shod — the stone stairs up to the tower base are worn down from many hundreds of years of soldiers' boots, and the ladder-climb to the top is both vertiginous and claustrophobic. Once there, though, the views are breathtaking.

Both Sestola and Fanano have various places to eat, from street food to pizzerias to more upscale dining. For today, though, we head back north, retracing our steps along the river before crossing it and taking yet another twisty road into the forested hills. We reach **Zocca**, a modest town with no great castle and no monumental history. What it does have, sitting on an unassuming commercial street across from a tire shop, is **Osteria dal Cinon**. Flowering vines and other plants envelop the front patio, creating a lovely little garden refuge from the road.

Chestnuts — Castagne

Chestnuts are a staple in many regions of Italy. Those from the slopes of Monte Amiata in Tuscany are highly regarded and IGP designated. Giving Amiata's chestnuts a run for their money, though, are the chestnuts of the forested foothills of the Apennine Mountains in central Emilia-Romagna. This region, the *fascia della civiltá del castagno* ("chestnut civilization zone") enjoys the ideal altitude to produce excellent chestnuts, hence the historical dependence on this natural bounty. *Castagne* replace wheat (which can't grow in these higher regions) in making flour, which is used in many recipes, from soups to desserts.

This excellent restaurant has been in the same family for generations, preparing old recipes with quality local ingredients. The owners take extreme care in choosing all the best items from neighboring organic farms and vineyards. Everything here is made fresh and in house; the *cameriere* will give detailed, passionate, and proud explanations about the food they are offering and the ingredients that go into it. Their classic dish, typical in the region, is *anolini in brodo* — little *prosciutto*-filled *tortellini* in a light broth. One of the occasional daily specialties is a chicken leg quarter, slow roasted for many hours and then finished in a hot oven. The result is a crispy, crunchy skin encasing the deliciously juicy meat inside. (This was served with a dollop of *piccante* sauce that the server warned us was extremely spicy. It wasn't, at least to our southern-U.S. palates. It was tasty, though.) The desserts here are also handmade and delicious, like their sweet yogurt parfait with local, seasonal berries. Cinon also offers several homemade *liquori*, such as walnut, peach, and orange, to quaff after your meal. If you have too many of these, you can walk it off with a quick visit to the nearby Chestnut Museum.

Osteria Cinon represents the very best of what

food in this region can be. Whether it's the carefully-selected local mushrooms on the *bruschette*, or the chicken from the poultry farm down the street, or the hand-picked chestnuts from the surrounding woods, or the perfectly crafted fresh pastas, or the grass-fed beef, or the fresh cream from the dairy farm

down the hill. The people here know exactly what they're eating, and they love it — and with good reason.

WHERE TO STAY

Castello di Serravalle

Corte di Ca' Bosco ★★ $

Modest, clean rooms set on a hillside above town. Ask for the room with the private patio, the room itself is very modest but it has full, exclusive use of a very large covered patio where you can have a glass of wine and enjoy the sunsets. The real treat here is the great restaurant downstairs. Enjoy a day of sightseeing, then return to the pastoral paradise at night to unwind and have a great meal.

http://www.cortedicabosco.it

Vignola

Caffé-Pasticceria Gollini ★★★ $

Closed Mondays and August. Open every other day from 8:00-12:30 and 3:30-7:30.

http://www.tortabarozzi.it/pasticceria.htm

Castello di Serravalle

Corte di Ca' Bosco ★★★★ $$

Patrons drive to this rural restaurant/hotel all the way from Bologna to enjoy the grilled meats, expertly cooked over an outdoor wood grill. Convivial, casual, fun atmosphere, you're invited to the party.

Closed Mondays. Open for dinner only, except Sunday lunch.

http://www.cortedicabosco.it

Zocca

Osteria dal Cinon ★★★★ $$

Excellent restaurant in the same family for generations. All food and wine sourced from local farms and vineyards, with a focus on sustainable, organic fare. Try the house-made liqueurs for dessert.

Closed Tuesdays and Wednesdays, reservations by phone only.

http://www.osteriadalcinon.com

Vignola

Castle of Vignola ★★★★

Free entry! Closed Mondays. Open in spring/summer from 9:00-12:00 and 3:30-7:00. Open in fall/winter from 9:00-12:00 and 2:30-6:00. Sundays and holidays same hours except opens at 10:30am.

http://www.fondazionedivignola.it

Monteveglio

Abbey of Monteveglio ★★

Open every day except during meal times and masses.

http://www.emiliaromagnaturismo.com/en/apennines-and-nature/parks/monteveglio.html

Fanano

Chiesa di San Silvestro ★★

Open Monday-Saturday 10:00-6:00 and Sunday 11:00-6:00.

Sestola

Castle of Sestola ★★★★ $

Entry 5€.

Open every day in July and August from 10:00-12:00 and 3:00-7:00, same hours on festival days. In other months, open upon request. The Mechanical Instruments Museum offers a demonstration of the instruments at 11am.

http://www.castellidimodena.it/page.asp?IDCategoria=287&IDSezione=5884

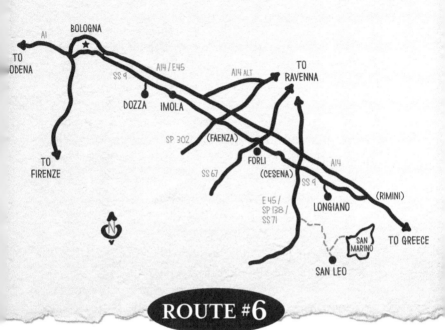

ROUTE #6

East of Bologna

Castles, Wine, and Wall Art

Our last route wanders the Romagna region to the east. We'll visit a village whose painted walls make it a free open-air art exhibit; choose tastes from among all the wines of the ER region in the cellar of an 800-year-old fortress; visit ancient medieval towers used by the Nazis as prisons; and eat in a 13th-century subterranean Monastic cantina.

We travel now to the southeast, past the ancient and beautiful city of Bologna, and into the Romagna territory of the Emilia-Romagna. Here, as we draw nearer to the Adriatic coast (even while still in sight of the Apennines), we discover more frequent seafood items on the menus, as well as the usual goodies for which Emilia-Romagna is famous. The pastas here have different names but are every bit as delicious: *strozzapetti*, *passatelli*, *nidi*, *garganelli*, *tortellacci*, *cappeletti*. Rather than the fizzy dry *lambrusco* of Emilia, the predominant wines here are the rich, dry Sangiovese red, and the sparkling, light but sweet Pignoletto.

We begin in charming **Dozza**, less than an hour to the southeast of Bologna. A well-preserved medieval walled village complete with a fortress at its peak, Dozza is a typical Italian hill town but for one element: It is the home of the "*Biennale del Muro Dipinto*" — the Biennial Exhibition of the Painted Wall. Every two years, artists travel to Dozza to paint artwork on the walls, decorating nearly every building with mural art in all styles, giving the town a truly unique feeling combining antiquity and modernity.

Dozza is quite small, with two long, main streets; plan to spend time walking them at different hours of the day, taking in the murals under various light conditions.

Dozza's **Rocca Sforzesca**, built in the 13th century and updated periodically over the course of the following few centuries, is laid out to show the high life in the Renaissance: Bedrooms with art and elaborately frescoed walls and ceilings; displays of clothing from the era; sitting rooms with huge fireplaces; the armament room, displaying various weapons of war; and an extensive kitchen equipped with all manner of

cooking tools and devices for pressing olives, grinding grains, and making *salumi*. The top floor houses various temporary art installations, sometimes modern ones; and of course, below ground there are dungeon rooms with inscriptions by the despondent prisoners over the centuries.

Sangiovese

In the Romagna, the eastern portion of ER, the default wine is the rich red Sangiovese. This is the same grape that is blended in famous Tuscan wines such as Chianti and Brunello; but here they produce Sangiovese di Romagna DOC (Denominazione di Origine Controllata — see Route 1). The name Sangiovese comes from the Latin words for "blood of Jupiter". Jupiter is the Roman version of Zeus, ruler of the gods; this more than anything shows the place that sangiovese has in the historic culture of the people here.

The bottom floor houses the **Enoteca Regionale Emilia Romagna**. This extensive shop, in what would have been the castle's vaulted storerooms, sells virtually every wine made in the Emilia-Romagna region, as well as grappa and even a few artisanal beers. Tastings are scheduled from time to time, run by highly trained *sommelieri*; check their schedule, or just ask "*Quando é la prossima degustazione?*" They also sell a few local foodstuff curiosities,

like chocolates infused with balsamic vinegar of Modena.

Dining options in this tiny town are many. **Albergo Ristorante Cane** is attached to a nice hotel, and has a large valley-view *terrazza* that makes for a great dinner setting. (The interior is dated and too-brightly lit to be romantic, but the food is good from any table.) Their offerings are regional standards; they usually have a seasonal prezzo fisso (fixed price) menu option. One specialty of the house is *pollo alla diavola*, a chicken dish whose 40-minute preparation time is well worth the wait.

Up the street next to the castle is another great dining spot: **Ristorante La Scuderia**. The front of the restaurant is also a bar, open early in the morning till late at night, serving coffees, pastries, wine

and aperitifs. There is a covered outdoor patio facing the castle, and also a cozy dining room in the back, much decorated with antique equestrian equipment (*scuderia* means "stable"). Pastas are handmade, like their *passatelli* (thick, ridged hand rolled pasta); also popular is fried polenta with *squaquerone*, a locally common,

soft tangy cheese. *Secondi* include a *pollo alla diavolo* and a housemade sausage. Plan on finishing your meal with samples of their housemade liqueurs — one of basil, and the other juniper. All in all, we found this food to be the best within the town walls of Dozza.

A mere five-minute drive west (or a half-hour walk) takes us up into the countryside to **Ristorante Monte del Re**. The restaurant is part of an upscale resort hotel complex built in a renovated Franciscan monastery — St. Francis himself is said to have placed a wooden cross at the church here in the 13th century. This is one of our "Destination Restaurants". The dining room has a formal atmosphere, and it is not open for lunch. However, the same menu is served downstairs in the much more casual cantina, a centuries-old wine cellar that still serves as such for the restaurant, but today also holds a few tables for lunch guests. The room is small, stone-walled, and circular, with an arched ceiling that creates some very unusual sound properties — certain points in the cavern acoustically correlate to others, so someone across the room whispering might sound as if they are right in your ear. The food here is based on tradition but with a distinctly modern twist, like a soft-boiled egg with a light breadcrumb crispy crust, its amazing orange-colored yolk cooked perfectly, on a bed of wilted spinach and topped with white truffle. Meat dishes include some fresh seafood (the mountainous surroundings make it easy to forget that we are close to the Adriatic Sea) and are finely prepared, like the delicate turbot fillet with thinly sliced grilled porcini mushrooms;

some artistically constructed potato-ribbon-wrapped scampi; and a pork loin cooked in milk with a delicious sauce of raisins and pine nuts. Don't miss their house-made desserts, like their robiola cheese tart dressed with a sauce of local berries and red wine. Monte del Re creates an unforgettable and incredibly delicious meal in a romantic setting. Reservations for lunch are advisable, as the cantina has only a few tables.

Just 10 kilometers east from Dozza is the much larger town of **Imola**, a town known for its distinctive blue ceramics as well as for its status as the unofficial western border of the Romagna region. It has been an agricultural market town since the Roman era; today it is the seat of the Ferrari Autodrome, a destination for Formula One racing enthusiasts.

Since we see little difference between auto racing and everyday driving in Italy, we prefer to occupy ourselves with the historical sights here. Imola's centro has an impressive Duomo, the **Basilica di San Cassiano**, built in the 13th century in blocky, Baroque style. A few blocks away is the town's real sight — the **Rocca Sforzesca**, built in the Middle Ages and updated massively in the Renaissance under the rule of the powerful Sforza family. The castle has odd hours, but a little advance planning will result in a private tour, given enthusiastically and proudly by one of the retirees who volunteer as guides. The edifice sits in the center of town surrounded by green space, which accentuates its imposing profile: Huge, squat, square, with round towers at every corner, and the remains of other towers from earlier versions of the fortress. It was once surrounded by a moat; now the moat is dry, offering a cross-section view of the rocky underpinnings of the structure.

A full visit to the castle takes a good couple of hours. The stones in the walls here saw a great deal of warfare over the centuries: Many displays of armaments and weapons of war fill several of the rooms of the castle, as well as many works of art depicting various battles and conflicts. Perhaps most famous is the episode in which the great

Duchess of Milan, Caterina Sforza, was imprisoned here when the Pope's son Cesare Borgia took the city in 1499, part of the great power struggles between the Borgia Pope and the various city-states of Italy. The fortress was used in relatively modern times as well — Mussolini's forces used it to house political prisoners before and during WWII. Some of their names were left behind, scratched into the dungeon walls alongside those of prisoners from centuries earlier. A visit to the display of "interrogation" apparatuses here makes it painfully clear that this must have been a quite unpleasant place to be incarcerated.

Today, the castle is used for much happier purposes: Weddings and other events are commonplace, as are the summertime movie showings in the courtyard. A few of the interior buildings, not open to the public, house the *Accademia Pianistica Internazionale*; as visitors go about their tour they can hear the piano students practicing.

For an excellent lunch here, find **Osteria di Vicolo Nuovo**. Tucked down a little side street (in fact *vicolo* means "little street"), this restaurant is owned by two friends, Ambra and Rosa, who opened the place in 1984. The outside is covered in lush ivy, and the 17th-century interiors are warm, cozy and inviting. This is a popular destination for locals, in part because they offer an inexpensive and unusual lunch special, consisting of salad, pasta, and vegetable all on one plate. We joked that it looked a bit like an Italian bento box.

Alla carta options are many and excellent, including a beautiful roasted artichoke with big shavings of *parmigiano*, accompanied by a savory *parmigiano* ice cream on a salty, buttery cracker. (We're in Romagna now, far from Parma; but the importance of *parmigiano reggiano* cheese is still paramount.) Seasonal soups are on offer as well, like an autumnal  potato and chick pea soup. Pastas are also made according to what's seasonal and fresh, such as their delicious (and generous) plate of artichoke-filled lasagna. Delicious house-made sausages with roast potatoes are among the options for *secondi*. Owner Ambra speaks to all the diners as if they are family, and she graciously sees to it that everyone has everything they need.

If you're looking to stock up your larder instead of eating out, seek out the small farm store **Azienda Fiorentina di Sopra**. Here, surrounded by farm-lands just north of the Imola *centro*, you can buy directly from the farm: produce, nuts, honey, jams (some unusual combinations as well, like zucchini

with mint and vanilla-apple), fruit juices, and wine of their own production. For those who like farm-to-table cooking, it doesn't get any better than buying directly from the farmer, getting to meet him and seeing the farm itself. As of autumn 2014, there is one particular rooster here who will follow you around like a puppy begging for treats, so buy an extra apple to feed him chunks if you are so inclined. Alternatively, ask the guys at the farm if they happen to have a special sale on *carne di gallo*.

Driving farther east, we come to the large town of Forli, another stronghold of Caterina Sforza. At the south edge of the centro is the 14th-century **Castello Ravaldino**, where Caterina's forces repelled those of Borgia in their early struggles. Today a large part of it is used as a prison, so visiting the interior is not particularly desireable. Nearby is the Museum of San Domenico; its large parking lot is a good place to leave the car to explore Forli's historic *centro*.

Two churches here are of special interest: The city's *duomo*, **Cattedrale di Santa Croce**, contains a sacred relic, a drawing of the Madonna on paper that was inexplicably spared after a fire in the 1400s. A chapel within the church holds the remains of Marcolino Amanni. a beloved mystic figure of Forli from the 14th century. A few blocks away, the old and narrow streets give way to the wide-open **Piazza Saffi**, the town square. Dominating the *piazza* is the church and bell tower of the **Abbey of San Mercuriale**, named for a 5th-century saint from Forli. The impressive church houses artifacts that speak to this ancient heritage, though most of it is newer — only 800 years old or so.

Near the aforementioned museum is one of our favorite lunch spots: **Osteria San Domenico**. The guys here serve up traditional Romagnese cuisine with flair and pride in a friendly, modern setting. Their menu reflects the season; one summer favorite was their *radicchio e bruciatelli*, a local dish of red lettuces topped with crispy pancetta (think bacon!) cooked in a little balsamic vinegar. Pastas are house-made; they also offer *piatti di giorno* — plates that aren't on the menu — so be sure to ask for the specials.

On the way east out of town on the SS9, do yourself a favor and turn right at the "Aeroporto" roundabout. There, across from the Super A&O supermarket, is the hip little **Le Conserve Bio Gelateria**. This is artisanal food at its best: Homemade in the back room — you can see them working through big panes of glass — the *gelato* here is made with all fresh, seasonal, and organic ("*biologico*") ingredients. Though it's a hip, modern place that contrasts with the ancient sights of the city, it exemplifies what's best about eating local.

Continuing our eastward path, we make our way past the little hill town of Longiano. We're now just 20 kilometers from the Mare Adriatico, but we're still surrounded by forested hills and rolling farmlands.

We'll return to explore Longiano in great

detail, but for now we drive south, again climbing into the Apennine foothills. We cross the Rubicon (not the momentous event it once was of old) and head to the twin hill towns of San Leo and San Marino. Legend has it that, back in the 3rd or 4th century A.D., two stonecutter friends came west from their jobs building the city walls in coastal Rimini. As members of an obscure cult called Christianity, they had been harassed and persecuted, so their zeal to spread the word led them into the hills of the Romagna to found two settlements. Marino founded what became the Republic of San Marino, which is its own country entirely within the borders of Italy. It is beautiful, old, and today heavily geared towards tourism, so we give it a pass. Instead, we head to the settlement founded by Marino's friend Leo, a little farther inland on a dizzying cliff protrusion that overlooks the valleys of the Marecchia and Mazzocco Rivers. This became the village, military outpost, and later fortification of **San Leo**, a town that seems to have erupted out of the rock itself.

Everything here is stone (fitting, considering the occupation of the supposed town father), and its relative inaccessibility has allowed the town to stay small and retain its ancient historic vibe. Dante Alighieri resided here for a time, and is said to have modeled his concept of Purgatory after San

Leo. A plaque in the town square commemorates this claim to fame. Driving across the mountain bridge and through the old town gate into the center feels like you've just entered some set piece of a medieval drama — you're surprised not to see helmeted guards atop the gate tower, shouting "Who goes there?!" (Or rather, "*Chi viene?!*") The streets are all cobblestones worn from centuries of use, and these stones blend into the many ancient buildings. At the end of town is the **Duomo di San Leo** and its adjacent bell tower, built in the 12th century on the remains of an earlier religious site. These edifices seem to have sprung out of the living rock; some of the cathedral's interior pillars are in fact bare, uncarved rock at their bases. Others, incredibly, have Roman-era capitals for their bases — a truly ancient application of the notion

Fare la scarpetta with Piada

The Italians have a term for using a piece of bread to mop up the remnants when finishing a soup or a pasta dish: Fare la scarpetta — literally, "to make the little shoe". Piada, common in the Romagna region, works for this as well as any other; it's a flatbread cooked in a terra cotta dish. But the piada (or piadina) can be a meal in itself: Folded and stuffed with an assortment of ingredients (prosciutto, mozzarella, and arugula is a standard combination), it is delicious, and it's a popular street food as well as being served in restaurants all over the region.

of "reduce/reuse/recycle". The crypt below the altar contains artifacts from as far back as the 6th century, including the inscribed cover of San Leo's sarcophagus. It reads, in part (and in Latin), "This is my rest for ever and ever; I live here because I prefer it". Taken together with the adjacent **Pieve di Santa Maria Assunta**, the area around the Duomo and its tower is reminiscent of a smaller (and much older) version of Pisa's Campo dei Miracoli. This one, though, doesn't sit comfortably on a lush green lawn; rather, it juts out of a hilltop as if it had been thrust through the rock from underground. (Also, the tower is straight.) The Pieve is even older than the cathedral, with sections dating back to the 8th century. The crypt holds a shrine to Santa Maria; the rooms are kept quite dark at times, even in the daylight hours, making it challenging even for a skeptic to walk the echoing, ancient aisles and steps without feeling... something.

Facing the town square is the **Museo di Arte Sacra**, housed in a 16th century palace commissioned by the Medici family. Its collection of sacred art from throughout the centuries is especially poignant here, since San Leo and San Marino (the actual guys, that is) played a vital role in encouraging the spread of Christianity in the area during those uncertain early centuries.

The **Rocca di San Leo** (built in the 15th century) looms over the entire valley from its perch on the mountain cliffs, looking like the unassailable fortress lair of some evil Bond villain. One corner of the fortress sticks out of the rock like a ship's prow; the other end sports two huge round towers. The upper keep of the castle was built first as a fortified residence; the towers and wall came a bit later, creating the almost impregnable structure we see today. This rocky promontory was a site of military importance since the Romans built an outpost on it two millennia ago, and it is easy to see why: It commands sweeping views of the countryside in all directions.

The castle currently houses several galleries of art; displays of weaponry and armaments through the centuries, up through and including World War Two; and of course the obligatory series of frightening torture rooms and oppressive prison cells. Of particular note

is the *Pozzetto Cagliostro*, or Cagliostro's Well: This is a small VIP prison cell accessible only through a trapdoor in the ceiling. Count Cagliostro, an infamous alchemist, freemason, forger, mystic, womanizer, philanthropist and swindler of the

18th century, was originally sentenced for his crimes to rot in the Castel Sant'Angelo in Rome. After an escape attempt, the Pope had him relocated to San Leo's *rocca* (which had by then become mainly a prison) and literally thrown into this most final of resting places. His cell, unlike the rest of the cells in the castle, had a window; though narrow, it overlooked the Duomo and the Pieve (church) below the castle. No doubt his jailers thought this to be fitting, as one of his many alleged crimes was heresy. The town is regarded now as not just a religious pilgrimage site but also an artists' retreat of sorts. Consequently it has quite a few galleries where artists and craftsmen ply their wares —

ceramics, woodwork, paintings, and more. Food culture is also well represented, including a butcher whose meat is locally sourced, a baker making fresh goodies daily, and several wine shops. **La Bottega di Luca**, just a few doors up the hill from the town gate, is a great source for local products, including wine, *salumi*, jams, bread, and cheese. Their specialty cheese is their own *formaggio alla fossa*, a cave-aged *pecorino* (sheep-milk cheese) unique to this producer. It is seasoned underground for months covered in leaves of a hazelnut tree. Try this specialty with a bit of the local honey. You can pick up all the makings of a great picnic here before hiking up to the Rocca to enjoy your goodies with a great view. Or stop on the way up the hill and eat at **Ristorante Locanda la Rocca**, where in the off-season the cheerful host Ivo waits the tables and does all the cooking himself. The place is reminiscent of a medieval dining hall where warriors should be drinking out of wineskins, with stone walls and large timbers supporting the vaulted ceilings. The food is all made in-house, including a great *tortellini* stuffed with spinach and ricotta with a sauce of seasonal vegetables. During our visit in November, Ivo explained that this "vegetable" sauce consisted of beans, sausage and pancetta. We looked at him quizzically; he shrugged and said, "Those *are* our winter vegetables…"

Ivo's establishment is a *locanda*, one of a handful of places in San Leo that offers rooms for those wishing to stay and explore the town further. For us, though, we must depart and make our way back north to **Longiano** as promised. Longiano is a tiny walled village in the woods, topped with a modest castle and watchtower. Just outside the walls is a single short street of shops and restaurants, as well as three churches: the Santuario del Santissimo Crocifisso and the Collegiate Church of San Cristoforo, and the former Basilica di San Giuseppe, which is now the civic **Museo di Arte Sacra** (museum of sacred art). Across from the

churches is the 19th century **Teatro Petrella**, noticeably similar in design to the Verdi's famous theatre in Busseto.

The town's 11th century **Castello Malatestiano** was one of the seats of the ancient and immensely powerful Malatesta family. Today it is home to a large modern art collection run by the Tito Balestra Foundation. Balestra was a local poet and arts advocate; one room is dedicated to portraits of him. Also on display are a few sketches by Matisse and Chagall, and works by many Italian artists from the past century, notably Vespignani and some particularly disturbing sketches by Zancanaro.

Beneath the castle hill are tunnels from the Second World War. The town, due to its strategic hilltop position, was the target of Allied air raids; these tunnels provided shelter and storage space for the citizens and for whatever military personnel were garrisoned here.

Excellent lodging can be found at the family-run **B&B Corte dei Turchi**, housed in a 16th-century building inside the town walls, just inside the north gate. Owner and innkeeper Massimo is extremely friendly and cheerfully encourages visitors to get the most out of their stay in this great little town. (His wife's family is Turchi, one of the town's old and influential families.) The rooms are clean and nicely appointed; little apartments and suites are available at a shockingly low rate. Breakfast is an extensive continental offering, including several goodies from local bakers. It is served in an ancient room that is like a small museum on its own, with many old-fashioned kitchen implements and other artifacts from centuries.

A small town, Longiano has just a few restaurants to speak of. For a simple meal, try the **Enoteca Stuzzicheria**, on the street just outside the town walls. *Stuzzicheria* refers to a place that serves small plates rather than full meals; nevertheless, it's hard to imagine not leaving here stuffed. They offer a few handmade pastas as well as a selection of pizzas, which are large and only cost around 6-8 Euro. They also have a large selection of artisanal beers made in Italy, a perfect accompaniment to the pizza.

The place that is considered by the locals to be the best (*"il ottimo!"*) is **Ristorante dei Cantoni**, located just steps away from the castle. Here you will find high-quality traditional dishes of the Romagna. They take pride in offering only the best, locally-sourced foods — even their pastas are made from flour from a local miller. A glance at their menu first offers *sfizi*, "whims" of the chef made from what's fresh, like the *piadine* (typical oven-baked flatbread) served with local cheeses (like the popular *squaquerone*) and their own *salumi*. Pastas and *secondi* are made with local meats and seafood, including some items that were caught or hunted that very morning. Desserts are freshly made and delicious, and some are served *al cucchaio*, "by the spoon" — that is, a series of tastes of various cremes with nuts, berries, or honeys from the area. Cantoni is indeed the ultimate in high-quality, fresh, local food presented in the finest traditional style; but this philosophy of cuisine is not hard to discover all over Emilia-Romagna, if one knows where to look and is willing to drive down the little roads.

Dozza

Albergo Ristorante Cane ★★★ $$

Hotel and restaurant with 3 floors and clean, airy rooms, as for a room with a view and you'll get one with lovely views over the valley. Free parking in the large parking lot below, which is accessed without entering the town (a big plus because the town can be driven in by residents only).

http://www.ristorantecanet.it

Longiano

B&B Corte dei Turchi ★★★ $

Small B&B offering a few rooms, including one larger apartment. Very clean and homey, also unbelievably affordable. Full kitchen in the apartment if you wish to cook your own meals. Free parking nearby. The B&B is just steps away from the Castle of Longiano. Continental breakfast is served in the breakfast room on the ground floor. Owner Massimo is extremely friendly and welcoming.

http://www.cortedeiturchi.it

WHERE TO EAT

Dozza

Albergo Ristorante Cane ★★ $$

Large restaurant on the ground floor of the Hotel Cane. In warmer months the restaurant has a very extensive, multi-level patio outside dripping with flowers for al fresco dining. Service is formal but friendly; pastas are handmade.

http://www.ristorantecanet.it

Ristorante La Scuderia ★ ★ ★ $$

Restaurant and bar at the top of town across from Dozza's Rocca. Delicious, handmade food, the best within the walled town. Try the house specialty, "pollo alla diavola". Service is casual and friendly in a warm, cozy environment. Finish off your meal with their own liqueurs made in house — try the juniper ("ginepro"). Closed Tuesdays.

http://www.ristorantelascuderia.com/en/-index.php

Ristorante Monte del Re ★ ★ ★ ★ $$$

Hands down, the best food in the area. Upscale, inventive new takes on traditional recipes. Upstairs is the more formal dining room, where service is also very formal. However, if you want to get the exact same food in a more casual environment, ask for a table in the Enoteca downstairs. It's quite a few steps down to the ancient wine cellar, but it's worth it. The atmosphere is cozy and romantic, and the food is absolutely stellar.

http://www.montedelre.it/?lang=en

Imola

Osteria di Vicolo Nuovo ★ ★ ★ ★ $$

Very popular with locals, Vicolo Nuovo is owned by two friends who are ever present in the kitchen and dining room. Ambra and Rosa love their work and the love comes through on the plate. Reservations are a must as the 17th century dining room fills up quickly.

http://www.vicolonuovo.it

San Leo

Ristorante Locanda la Rocca ★★★ $$
Located on the path on the way up to la Rocca, this cozy restaurant is well worth a meal. Pastas are handmade, as are desserts. Ask the owner for recommendations, he speaks great English and is happy to oblige. If you are here in the off season you may find that he is your waiter as well as your chef.

Longiano

Enoteca Stuzzicheria ★★ $
On the main street just a few blocks away from the castle is this little Enoteca, which is also a Birreria (beer purveyor). Pastas and pizzas only. For a low-key meal for those that might like to try some of the new Italian artisanal beers.

Closed Thursdays. Dinner only.

Ristorante dei Cantoni ★★★ $$

Just steps away from the Castle of Longiano. Restaurant serving traditional dishes of the Romagna, with ingredients sourced from local farms. Extensive wine list. A great place to go if you want to familiarize yourself with the cuisine of the area.

Closed Wednesdays.

http://www.ristorantedeicantoni.it

Dozza

Enoteca Regionale Emilia Romagna ★★★★ $

Enoteca located in the ground floor of the Castle of Dozza. Very extensive wine collection, meant to include the best of what all Emilia Romagna has to offer. Liqueurs and some artisanal products (e.g. grains, jams, chocolates and biscotti) can also be found here.

Open Tuesday-Friday 9:30-1:00 and 2:30-6:00. Saturdays and festivals from 10:00-1:00 and 3:00-6:00. Sundays from 10:00-1:00 and 2:30-6:45. In the summer closes 30 minutes later.

On Sundays there is a wine bar which is open from 2:30-6:30 in winter and 3:00-6:00 in summer.

http://www.enotecaemiliaromagna.it/en

Imola

Azienda Fiorentina di Sopra ★★★ $
Farm shop just northwest of Imola selling products of its own making including wine, juices, produce, baked goods, nuts and honey. Many of the jams and salsas are quite unusual and inventive.

http://www.fiorentinadisopra.it

San Leo

La Bottega di Luca ★★ $
Located just steps away from the town gate, Bottega di Luca is the only producer and seller of the excellent pecorino which is aged in hazelnut leaves. Jams, honeys, wine and liqueurs of local production can also be found here.

Dozza

Rocca Sforzesca ★★★ $
A 13th-century castle displaying art, armaments, and culture throughout the centuries, now most importantly guarding the great treasure of the Enoteca Regionale Emilia Romagna in its cellars.

Entry 5€, 3€ for students. Closed Mondays,

December 25 and January 1. Open Tuesday-Saturday 10:00-12:30 and 2:30-7:00. Open Sundays 10:00-1:00 and 2:30-6:00. In summer, the Rocca is open for an additional 1.5 hours in the evening.

Imola

Rocca Sforzesca ★★★★ $

An impressive castle in the middle of town, showing a vast cross-section of history, from medieval bastion to Mussolini's tyranny.

Entry €3.50.

Open Saturdays 3:00-7:00. Sundays 10:00-1:00 and 3:00-7:00. Tuesdays-Fridays open 9:00-1:00 by appointment only. Other times, may be open by appointment if requested.

San Leo

Duomo di San Leo ★★★

This ancient cathedral seems to have grown right out of the rock. Its bell tower is closed for visitors but the bells chime now and then.

Hours: 9:30-12:30, 2:30-6:00

Pieve di Santa Maria Assunta ★★★

Not for the faint of heart — we were sure that something was lurking in the shadows in this hallowed 8th century site.

Hours: 9:30-12:30, 2:30-6:00

Rocca di San Leo ★★★★ $$

The climb through the woods from San Leo to this cliff-castle is short but strenuous; the views are as grand as the castle itself.

Hours: Monday-Friday 9:30 AM — 5:15 PM, Sat/Sun 9:30-6:15

Tickets: €8. Combo ticket w/Sacred Art Museum: €10.

Museo di Arte Sacra ★★ $

This museum is worthwhile just to see the Medicean Palace, as well as the art collection.

Hours vary wildly — check the TI office next door.

Tickets: €3.

Longiano

Castello Malatestiano ★★ $

Much of the castle in Longiano is now used as a gallery of artists from the past two centuries, including sketches by Matisse and Chagall.

Closed Monday.

Open 10-12 and 3-6,

Tickets: €3

APPENDIX 1

EATING AND DRINKING

List of foods to make sure you eat/drink in Emilia-Romagna

Emilia-Romagna is the breadbasket region of Italy, and is the source of some of the country's hallmark ingredients: *Prosciutto* ham from Parma, balsamic vinegar from Modena, the ubiquitous *parmigiano reggiano* cheese, and much more. Here are a few of the delicious typical foodstuffs to be found in the region:

Lambrusco — light, *vino rosso frizzante* (sparkling red wine), common in Emilia (central and western ER).

Pignoletto — sparkling *vino bianco* (white wine), common in Romagna (eastern ER).

Sangiovese — "Jupiter's blood", the standard red wine of the Romagna

Parmigiano reggiano — the iconic cheese, served in abundance on almost every plate.

Salumi — cold cuts of various types, including *salami*, *prosciutto*, *culatello*.

Prosciutto — ham; most famous is *prosciutto di Parma*. Two types, *cotto* (cooked) and *crudo* (cured, usually with salt and lots of months in a basement). Both are delicious.

Culatello — the "filet mignon" of *prosciutto*; the best cut, more difficult to prepare/season/age, and therefore more expensive, but worth it.

Torta fritta — fried bread pockets, usually served along with a plate of *salumi* and *parmigiano*

Tortelli — hand-made, stuffed pasta, very common in ER (tortellini, tortelloni vary in size), stuffed with cheese, meats, and/or vegetables.

Aceto balsamico — balsamic vinegar; the best is from the Modena area. If something has *balsamico di Modena* on it, get it.

Piada/piadina — a flat bread, common in the Romagna region, sometimes folded and stuffed with meats and cheeses.

Castagne — chestnuts, especially common in the forested hills and mountainous areas.

Liquori — liqueurs, usually distilled from herbs and/or fruits. Common in ER are *bargnolino* (made from berries from a thorn plant) and *nocino* (made from unripe walnuts). Different types of *grappa* are also widely available.

Other key dining terms

colazione, pranzo, cena — breakfast, lunch, dinner

prenotazione — reservation

tavola — dining table

carta — menu

aperitivo — a little drink before the meal

vino della casa — house wine

bicchiere — glass

bottiglia — bottle

carafe — carafe

barriche — barrel

fuori/dentro — outside/inside ("*Possiamo mangiare fuori?*" "Can we eat outside?")

digestivo — a little drink after the meal

Fatto in casa — made in-house

troppo cibo — too much food

sono pieno — I am full

non posso mangiare piu — I can't eat any more

OK, forse solo uno dolce — okay, maybe just one dessert

The Restaurant Experience

Restaurants have many names in Italy: *Ristorante, Osteria, Trattoria,* and *Locanda* are by far the most common.

The first thing that will happen at any restaurant is the *cameriere* bringing bread and asking what kind of *acqua* (water) you would like. This will always be bottled water, and can be *naturale* (flat) or *frizzante/gassata* (sparkling). Don't ask for tap water — this would be like asking for a drink out of the garden hose.

Bread will usually not come with butter or a dish of oil; it is meant to be used to soak up sauces on your plates. You'll see that a per-person *coperto* (cover charge) is indicated on the menu. This is typically a couple of bucks, and is meant to stand as a minimum service charge.

Meals are served in courses:

Antipasti — appetizers

Primi — pastas, soups or *risotto*

Secondi — meat dishes — this will be just meat; if you want a side dish, order a contorni

Contorni — vegetables, potatoes or salad

Dolci — desserts; occasionally this list will include a cheese plate

Cafe/digestivi — coffee (don't get a cappuccino!) or digestive liqueur, like an *amaro* or a *grappa*

Diners are not obligated or expected to order a dish from every course; we frequently skip either the pasta or the meat course. However, if you find yourself in an especially charming or romantic location, settle in for what we refer to as an "epic" meal.

Once you have a table, it's yours for the night. There will be no turnover or pressure for you to leave. It's generally considered very rude to put a bill on the table, so often the service staff is waiting for you at the end of a meal to approach them to ask for "*il conto*" (the bill).

Meals are slow, and there can be a good amount of time in between courses, as they are making your dish from scratch. If you want a faster meal, try a Panificio (sandwich shop), pizzeria, or bar, or grab a picnic lunch at a grocery store.

Most small-town restaurants are family-owned, and as a result they won't always adhere to their stated schedules. If one of their family members has a baby or a sudden medical need/wedding/vacation, they might not open up as usual. Be ready to improvise.

A note on tipping

After a meal, you'll need to ask for *il conto* (the check), as they won't try to bum-rush you out as they do in the States. Though it's not generally expected, we often leave a little something extra — usually somewhere between 10 and 20 percent — to show appreciation for good service.

Meal times and reservations

While reservations are not generally required, it's a good idea to have them, even in casual restaurants. Reservations can be made the same day, even an hour in advance. Basically you are just reserving a table and getting a head-start on the lunch rush. No ties/jackets are ever required at the places we recommend (though you are welcome to wear them if you like). Some of the restaurants we recommend are real mom-and-pop places, and some are upscale, but all will allow you to eat there wearing regular clothing (no Speedos/flip flops, however).

It's not unusual to make a reservation and then be the only people eating that day. Sometimes the reservation just insures that the restaurant opens at all. In the US if you saw an empty restaurant you'd know that was a sign of poor quality, but that is often not true in Italy, especially in very small towns. No reservations are required (or even possible) in pizzerias and small sandwich shops; reservations are only for sit-down restaurants.

Seatings for *pranzo* (lunch) generally happen no earlier than 12:30 and no later than maybe 2:00. Shoot for 1:00-1:30 to be safe. If you're looking for a place to eat at 2:30, you may be totally out of luck.

Cena (dinner) starts at maybe 7:30, and goes on until everyone is done eating. Again, if you wait much later than 9:00, they may turn you away, depending on how busy the place is.

Breakfasts: Some lodgings offer *colazione* (breakfast), which range from a full-service spread of meats, cheeses, fruits and breads to a packet of biscuits and a yogurt cup in the mini-fridge. We almost always skip it altogether; we like to say that if you need breakfast, you didn't do dinner right.

Bar Culture

Italy's main social scene is at the various neighborhood or roadside bars. This is where you get your coffee in the morning (or any time of day, really), your *aperitivo* before lunch, your drinks and such before or after dinner. Ask for a *café* and you'll get the tiny, very strong espresso. *Cappuccino*, with its frothy steamed milk on top, is typical in the mornings only, though they will make you one any time. Sometimes they will shorten the word "cappuccino" to the slang "cappucci".

Other common drinks:

Spritz Aperol (sweeter) or *Spritz Campari* (more bitter) are cocktails with prosecco; Campari and soda; *spremuta* (fresh squeezed orange juice, you'll see a machine behind the bar with a basket of oranges if they have this); café corretto (espresso mixed with grappa); prosecco; and of course wine. At the bar you can also buy a bottle of water (*naturale* for flat; *gassata* or *frizzante* for sparkling), which you can drink there or take on the road.

We've never seen anyone drinking cocktails like a martini or a cosmopolitan, though they could probably make one if requested. In the last few years many bars have begun to offer Italian-made artisanal beers.

The bar is a great place to try a shot of the endless varieties of Italian 'amari', or liqueurs. Ask for "*un amaro*", and just point to the one you'd like to try. Cynar (CHEE-nar) is made from artichokes, Montenegro from herbs, Averna is also made from herbs. It can be fun to give them a try, each will cost 2-4€. They will probably ask you if you want it with ice ("*con ghiaccio*").

If you order a cocktail (e.g. Aperol spritz, or an *amaro*), the bartender may also bring you a little dish of nuts or olives, tiny sandwich bites or other snacks. Those are free with your drink. If you're happy with the drink and service, it's nice to leave a Euro or two as a tip. (Note: baristas do not generally expect tips, but they always appreciate one.)

GENERAL TIPS FOR TRAVELING IN ITALY

Passports

Your US passport must be valid for six months after the last date of your trip. If your passport expires in October and your trip ends in May, you will not be able to board the plane.

If you need a new passport or need to renew your old one, the State Department recommends doing that at least 6 weeks in advance. We recommend 3 months, just to avoid the stress of frantically checking the mail every day. We also highly recommend applying for Global Entry, which will greatly expedite your time waiting in line at both ends of your trip.

Renting a car

International Driver's Licenses are required for foreign drivers in Italy. These can be purchased at AAA (even for nonmembers) for $15. You will also need your regular driver's license.

Snow tires or chains are now legally required between November 15 and April 15. This will often mean an additional fee from the rental company (to hire chains) if the car is not equipped with snow tires. You may not see any snow (we rarely have, after multiple winter trips) but nevertheless you are required to pay to be prepared. If you know it is going to snow, or if it starts to snow, you need to stop and get the chains on. Having not put chains on a car since 1980 or so, we don't love the idea either, but it's a small price to pay for a great trip (and to avoid a citation from the *Carabinieri*, the Italian state police). For more driving tips — from picking up the car to insurance to traffic signs to navigation to parking — check our website, **LittleRoadsEurope.com**, which includes many pictures and links.

Driving in Italy

People are often intimidated by driving in Italy. The drivers are often fast and aggressive, and American drivers may feel pressured to go faster by drivers who tailgate very closely. This is just a cultural norm in Italy — remember that it's not personal. If someone is following you too closely, look ahead for a place to pull over and let them pass easily. Usually they're not even paying attention to you, they just drive like this out of habit. If they are irritated at your slow speed, that's okay — once they pass you, you'll probably never have to see them again. Give them a little wave and cheerful "Ciao!" as they pass you by.

Tolls

The only toll roads are the Autostrada highways. Approaching a toll plaza, you'll see lanes marked in blue that say "*Carte*" (credit cards). You can use your credit card in the automated machines to get through. If you prefer to pay cash, look for the lanes marked with the pictures of money. Some of the toll plazas give you a "*biglietto*" — a ticket, like on the NJ Turnpike — upon exiting, you insert that before inserting your *carta* (credit card) to pay the toll.

Gas Stations

Filling up is usually easy enough, at one of the many service stations along the highways or in towns. Many of them have two lanes, one for "*Servizio*" and one "*Fai da te*" (do-it-yourself). The self-service is a little cheaper, but we usually opt for the service attendant in case there's some trick to the pumps. Ask for "*senza piombo*" (unleaded) or "*diesel*" (diesel), and tell him how much you want — a number of euro, or just "*al pieno*" (full). (And don't forget to say "*per favore*"!) If the weather is bad we usually tip the attendant a couple of bucks. Most of these places take credit cards, and you'll have to go inside their little office to pay. Sometimes the place is set up just like an American convenience store — just note the number of your pump and tell the clerks inside, and they'll ring you up.

Note: On Sundays, many if not all service stations are closed. In this event, some of them have auto-pay machines that take cash and, depending on the specific machine, some types of cards. These can be confusing, and for this reason we always avoid them altogether, making sure that on Saturday we have a full tank.

Money

Cash is king. Nearly all restaurants and hotels accept credit cards, but some still do not, so make sure you know before you buy. Bars will not accept cards — you will always need cash for that. Italians also have a deep love for exact change, and efforts on your part to produce exact change will be appreciated. They also have a love of small bills. Trying to buy a 1€ espresso with a 20€ note will garner you some dirty looks, and in small towns, they may not even have enough change for that.

Note: We've found that many places that do accept cards do not accept American Express, since their commission fees are so high. Mastercard and VISA are generally fine.

Check with your bank about international ATM withdrawal fees. We use ATMs ("*Bancomat*") there as needed, as the exchange rate is the same or close to what you will find at the airport. (Traveler's checks have gone the way of wooden dentures, so don't even ask.)

Exchange counters at the airport often offer "deals" that allow you to exchange unspent Euros on your trip back without fees. Alternatively, you can just keep track of your spending in general and work your way down to zero Euros at the end of your trip.

Wi-Fi

Free wi-fi is available at many B&Bs, restaurants and bars. You can call your phone company and have an international data package added for a month. That said, we recommend just using free wi-fi when you find it, or better yet, take a break from constantly being tethered to your phone. You'll be amazed at how much more you experience things around you when you are not focused on staring at a small screen.

Packing

It's impossible to overstate the importance of packing light for a good trip, for two reasons:

1) You want the most mobility and flexibility, so your focus is on experiencing the place you are visiting, and not managing the mound of stuff in your suitcase; and 2) the goal is to arrive with very little, and leave with bags laden down with all the goodies you'll find. Trust us, you'll be disappointed if you can't buy that bottle of oil or ceramic vase because you had to make room for your hairdryer/extra shoes/umbrella. We've traveled overseas dozens of times, and we offer extensive advice on packing smart on our website LittleRoadsEurope.com.

Language

Even in small towns you will often find plenty of English-speakers. Oftentimes you'll find people who want to practice their English by chatting with you. That said, we highly recommend starting your encounters with a bit of Italian. A simple "*buon giorno*" (good day), "*per favore*" (please), or "*grazie*" (thank you) goes a long way. It's easy to learn a few key phrases, and making the effort opens the door for making real connections with people. It's also important to remember that you are a guest in their country, and to treat people the way you would like to be treated.

A note on Visiting/Opening Hours

Opening hours for shops and sites are variable according to the season; but in general, most sites are open from mid-morning until lunchtime, and then reopen from the mid-afternoon until early evening. For most tourist sites (e.g., museums, castles), the last entry is 30-45 minutes before the actual closing time.

On festival days (of which there are many), shops and other businesses may be closed, but most tourist sites will be open (perhaps with varying hours). Look for paper signs plastered on walls for information that you'd normally expect to find on a website; while web presence is increasing, roadside flyers are still the most common form of advertising.

Lodging — What to Expect, What to Look For

Lodging in Italy is much less of the cookie-cutter experience you'll find in the US. In the large Italian cities you can find standard and also luxurious hotels that are like any you would find around the globe. In the smaller towns, though, chain hotels are nonexistent. Instead you'll find small, family run hotels and B&Bs. Sometimes a hotel will be called "Albergo", "Pensione", or "Locanda". A locanda is usually a hotel with a restaurant. B&Bs usually mean you'll have breakfast included, but that breakfast will never involve the eggs, waffles, bacon, and cinnamon buns that you would find at an American B&B. Italians eat very light breakfasts — we always say that if you need breakfast, you didn't do dinner right. At a typical B&B breakfast you'll find coffee, juice, breads (fresh or packaged) and jams, nutella, and maybe yogurt. We almost always skip these breakfasts and instead opt to eat at a nearby bar with the locals, where we take in the sights, smells and sounds of the day. If you intend to eat hotel breakfast, be sure to check if your B&B or hotel offers it free — sometimes there is an additional charge.

A few other things you likely won't find in a small town Italian hotel:

- hairdryers, irons and ironing boards, coffee service, room service
- mini fridge (these are becoming more common now, to our delight)
- TV and phone
- Air conditioning
- elevators
- large, nearby parking lots
- 24 hour concierge

Some of these may be there, but they are not ubiquitous as in American hotels.

You *will* find:

- religious art on the walls
- proprietors who live there or quite nearby, and know the area well
- stunning views
- peace and quiet

When we look for lodging, we are always looking for location. Sometimes we'll book a remote castle, which is not near any restaurants — in that case we may have picnic dinners to avoid driving at night, and also to spend the most time possible in a stunning fairytale location. Sometimes we'll book into a restaurant that has rooms upstairs, so we can eat "epic" meals and then roll ourselves up the stairs at the end of the night to sleep it off. Most often we book small, affordable places in or within walking distance to small walled towns, so we can park the car and leave it while we explore the town on foot. We always look for places that are going to give us a memorable, meaningful trip with a minimum of hassle.

A planning note

Many of the small places we list in this book are, to our knowledge, not listed anywhere else. We have made every effort to accumulate and update the information in this book; however, small businesses can shut down or be closed unexpectedly for illnesses, vacations ("*ferie*"), or just because they felt like it. Many of the places we list have websites and/or Facebook pages; we suggest you confirm their opening days/times before visiting to avoid disappointment. Without limit, we are not responsible for any distress, disappointment, or damage incurred by following this guide. However, if you do find information that you think could use updating, please let us know by contacting us via email at littleroadseurope@gmail.com.

Complete information on all our listings, including many more photos of sights, dishes, and lodgings we visit in this book, please visit us at http://www.LittleRoadsEurope.com.

Buon appetitio, e buon viaggio!

Thank you!

We hope you've enjoyed this book. For more information on the places we travel, please visit us at www.LittleRoadsEurope.com.

Interested in other regions of Italy? Check out our guide to Tuscany — find out how to visit this tremendously popular region, off the beaten path.

If you're thinking about a trip to Italy, consider our Itinerary Building Service. We design custom itineraries for clients based on our extensive travel experiences in Emilia-Romagna, the northern lakes regions, and Tuscany. Based on your preferences, we'll help you navigate these regions, make reservations, visit artisans, and give recommendations for a trip that is authentic, immersive, memorable and affordable. Start your vacation before you even leave and let us do the hard part!

~ Matt & Zeneba

Notes

Little Roads Europe

Notes